THE MONERO STANDARD

"We're not here for the income,
We're here for the outcome".

By

Michael Fitzgerald (@TheStoicCoiner)

Index

I would like to sincerely thank Cake Wallet from the bottom of my heart for sponsoring this book.

The contribution from Vik Sharma (@vikrantnyc)) and the Team at Cake Wallet allow the message to be spread to a level that would not be possible without them.

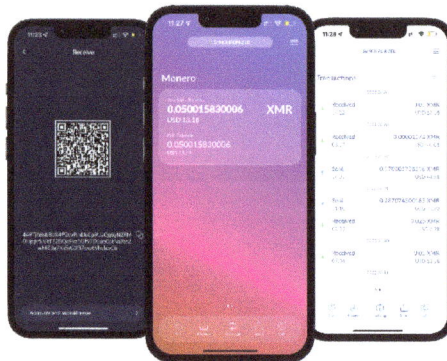

Cake Wallet is an open source, noncustodial wallet for Monero that focuses on ease of use. It has been around since early 2018.

Cake Wallet includes Cake Pay, a convenient way to spend XMR on goods and services.

Cake Wallet is available on Android and iOS.

Learn more at http://cakewallet.com

I would like to sincerely thank Neel Capital from the bottom of my heart for sponsoring this book.

The contribution from Namrata Sardar (@namsardar) and the team at Neel Capital allow the message to be spread to a level that would not be possible without them.

Neel Capital is a return-focused crypto asset investment firm that combines fundamental analysis with an active management approach.

Learn more at www.neelcapital.io

vi

I would like to sincerely thank MoneroNodo from the bottom of my heart for sponsoring this book.

The contribution from Douglas Tuman (@DouglasTuman) and the team at MoneroNodo (@MoneroNodo) allow the message to be spread to a level that would not be possible without them.

Nodo

MoneroNodo is an optimized plug & play node.

Nodo makes it easier than ever to support the Monero network by running a fully dedicated node and to use Monero in the most secure and private way.

Learn more and order one today at www.Moneronodo.com

Foreword

Society, in many ways, is on a very scary and questionable trajectory. We need functioning and freedom preserving money to fix these problems. Importantly, we need privacy in any functioning and freedom preserving money to fix those problems.

Why? Well, we explore that in this book.

This is what will set humanity free forever (believe it or not).

An "unfuckable" money destroys the predatory incentive systems upheld solely by fiat money and totally reshapes the current societal incentive systems in many areas from finance and politics to societal mobility and environmentalism.

Monero is more in line with the original goals and ambitions of Bitcoin/Cryptocurrency as were outlined by Satoshi Nakamoto in the Bitcoin whitepaper, literally titled "A peer to peer electronic cash system".

As the saying goes "Monero is what Bitcoin n00bs thought they bought"

We will also explore why Bitcoin is suboptimal in performing this role and why Monero, being a private money/cryptocurrency, is the best option we have for achieving a genuinely free and resilient peer to peer electronic cash system.

Ladies and gentlemen, I love freedom.

Without it, there is no point in living.

This book is for the people, for privacy and for freedom.

The information in this book will set you free and help you discover a new way of life.

Free from the manipulation uncovered in this book that you may have never previously considered possible.

That is the mission.

Without freedom, we are all dead anyway.

Chapter 1

The History of Money –

How did we get here?

Well really, truth be told. It would have been much better if I did not have to write this book at all, and by extension, it would be much better if there was no need for Monero at all.

To understand the purpose of this book, it is vitally important to go back in time and firstly understand what money actually is, so that we can understand how the problems in today's society are caused by money amongst other things.

Without this understanding, it would be difficult for one to be able to adequately put their finger on the problem and the solution.

Many think they know what money is, however, very few people actually understand what money is.

In a perfect world, we would be able to trust those in control of the money. If indeed there needed to be someone in charge at all (which there doesn't need to be).

In a perfect world, those in control would not debase and manipulate the monetary supply for their own personal macro or micro gains.

We have seen fiat money play out numerous times in history… always with more or less the same causes and certainly always with the same result in the end. Complete failure and disintegration of the civilization/empire that bears it.

But as we know, humans are fallible and humans are greedy, just to name a few flaws.

That is where Monero comes in to perform the function of a trustless & mathematically certain way to curb certain societal behaviours that have led to the manipulation and essential pillaging of many areas.

Areas from politics all the way to health.

If you are new to the decentralised money or just casual reader of this book, this new monetary system incentivises many positive changes in human and societal behaviour to a level you had probably never previously considered through the reconstruction of societies incentive structures. This is because as we know, money controls everything. Money makes the world go round as the saying goes. We will discuss this further in later chapters.

You will see why Monero and privacy is not negotiable in a truly free society .

As long as humans continue to be fallible and greedy, then there will always be a need for Monero and decentralised private money.

Speaking humbly, I think there is by now, a long enough track record to prove that humans will continue to be fallible.

If you think humanity is perfect and subsequently, that we can trust in central planning of monetary and power structures. I suggest you save your time, stop reading the book and go about your life as though this never happened. You probably need this book more than anyone, but you will first need to undergo fundamental experiences to show you that human power structures are indeed fallible in order to get anything from this book. There are millennia of history to back this up.

If you think humans can fix their thousands of years of fallibility, simply with human designed systems that rely on the fallibility of people, trust and "the greater good", then you need this book more than anyone.

Ok, you're still here. let's get into the history of money.

I don't want to explore the history of money on a level that is unnecessarily complicated. Rather we will focus on the fundamental concepts that will leave you with the knowledge set that is required to understand the following chapters in the book. Ultimately, what money actually is and the important role it plays in a society.

Whilst it's the characteristics of Monero vs other monies that give it its superiority, it's important to understand the history of money first, as you will not understand or at least not recognise the full significance of some concepts further down the track without understanding the history and the historical precedents that have led to a successful money.

So, let's explore, what is money?

Money and value, when you think about it, is just a made up concept. Money doesn't actually exist, there is no inherent money in the world and by extension, there is no inherent value in the world, all value is subjective. All value derives from our perception. Essentially, our monkey brain telling us what it does and doesn't value based on our real world preferences.

Money is just a word for assets that people commonly see as "valuable" that are used to exchange value on a scale the is socially recognisable.

Successful monies have historically needed to have 6 characteristics that ensure its position as the most apex money.

They are:

- Durability
- Portability
- Divisibility
- Fungibility
- Scarcity
- Acceptability

The money which best represents these 6 characteristics has historically speaking, been considered the most saleable form of money.

To break it down, Money is societies most saleable good that is used to exchange value.

Let's break down a bit further exactly what constitutes the each of these attributes that contribute to what becomes the most saleable good.

Durability

It doesn't take a genius to figure out that money needs to be durable.

Money needs to be able to withstand the elements as a starting point and ideally needs to be able to withstand all kinds of disasters, both natural and man-made.

Naturally, nothing in this world is indestructible. And just to clarify, it's not the most durable/dense asset or commodity that is considered money by default.

Durability is the characteristic that allows it to be a **store and transfer of value over time**, if the other characteristics which we will discuss are also met.

If money is perishable for example, it cannot be considered a good store of value. For example, wheat will rot after some time compared to gold, which is chemically stable and will not rot, decay or transform over time. Additionally, gold cannot be created or destroyed. This durability ultimately leads to its limited supply as well. You cannot destroy gold

As another example, other metals such as iron will rust over a given period of time, thus are not good "stores of value over time".

For the record, Monero is a unit of account stored on a decentralised private digital ledger, possibly one of the most durable pieces of technology the world has ever seen.

Resistant to all natural disaster, political regimes, attrition, and natural affects such as rot or evaporation.

The technical factors of this claim are incredibly nuanced. The nuance of my claim will be detailed further in chapter 6.

Portability

I won't dwell on this one. If you can't carry or port it to transfer value, then you can't use it as a medium of exchange, can you? Pretty obvious right, but still important to cover off.

To sum it up more formally, in addition to being a **store and transfer of value over time** as is determined by its durability, money also needs to be a **store and transfer of value over space**. Which is assessed by its portability.

Store and transfer of value over time & space. Two very important concepts for money that you need to keep in mind whilst determine what money is best.

Divisibility

The need for divisibility is one of the main proponents as to why paper money was first introduced.

Gold and silver were/are not very dividable, you would need a smelter or at best, tools, to divide gold and silver. Therefore, having redeemable paper notes backed by gold/silver gave an added layer of portability to gold and silver, which meant the market could value these paper notes as akin to money.

As one of my old boss' used to say, "if you want to buy a mars bar with gold, you cannot just shave off a piece of gold to pay for the mars bar."

You need a very specific amount of gold to pay for whatever you are purchasing. Usually, an impractically small amount. To divide gold into any given amount usually takes a large amount of cost, time and expertise to do so. This is why gold is not very portable, therefore it is hard for it to be used as an **effective** medium of exchange.

In this department, as mentioned, dollars are far superior as a medium of exchange because you can easily divide 1 dollar into 100 x 1 cent pieces.

To sum it up, any money needs to be easily dividable to all relevant amounts.

Uniformity/ fungibility

All money needs to be equal; this inherently seems like a simple concept however it is not necessarily as easy to decipher as it may appear.

Just to clarify, an example of what I mean:

- 1g Gold = 1g Gold,
- $1 bill = $1 bill
- 1 Monero = 1 Monero

To sum it up, the money needs to be identical.

This statement seems obvious however, this is why something like houses cannot be used as money.

Despite having almost universal value, 1 house doesn't equal 1 house simply because it's a house, right?

You can even extend this statement to commodities like apples. All apples are different sizes, shapes, colour. No matter how similar they are, they are all still different.

This is also why, for cash, we can use the example of drug money or money held by a celebrity.

If you know a money has for sure been used in shady dealings then you will be less likely to accept it because you won't want it tied to you, maybe you're sitting here saying you would still accept it but others would definitely be less likely to accept it, even if it were to change your behaviours, such as that you would want to get rid of that "drug money" first, then you can consider this as it being non desirable and not akin to 1=1.

Conversely, if you know a certain dollar bill for example had been used or held by a celebrity then you would probably be more likely to hold onto that dollar bill. In fact, it's likely that you could even sell that $1 bill for more than its face value, meaning that 1≠1.

Luckily, cash is not traceable. When you receive a dollar bill, you are almost certainly not going to know of its history. This means that cash is fungible. Moving into the digital age with the problems to solve that we will later discuss, a digital cash will also need to be fungible, exactly like cash is today.

As you will come to see later in the book, this reasoning of fungibility is the reason why Bitcoin cannot be used as an effective digital cash over a long period of time, it is not fungible. However, we will get into that later.

Limited supply

The quality of any money is also determined by what is known as "hardness". The phrase, despite the views of some, derives from how "hard" it is to create more of that money/ how hard it is to expand the monetary supply of that asset.

If something can be easily created or reproduced, many people will be able to easily obtain it, thus the purchasing power of that asset will decrease significantly, and amount of that money required to trade for goods and services will increase exponentially.

This is simply because people could just create it rather than having to provide genuinely valuable goods or services to the market in exchange for it. If you can create money out of thin air/easily, given the fact that you cannot create goods and services easily, it will lose its value significantly vs goods & services.

Game theory for a second... Let's use an example of digital credits as money.

If you have a virtual system where you can create money out of thin air for free, you and everyone else would create an infinite amount of "money", which would lead to an exponential increase in the monetary supply and thus the purchasing power of each unit would shrink to almost zero.

The lack of ability to easily create more is what drives the value of a money over long period of time.

In short, "Hardness" can be boiled down to how much work is required to produce more. Not how physically hard/dense the money is, as gold bugs will debate. In the same way they say "sound" in the sense that if you drop it, it makes a sound. ***Cough, Peter Schiff***

Money is essentially **proof of work**.

Acceptability

Of course, Network effect i.e., whether or not people accept it, is very important when it comes to adoption of a money.

It is, however, a variable.

The network effect it is not set in stone compared other characteristics such as divisibility, where something can categorically be considered divisible or not. As time goes on, gold does not become more divisible or easier to carry.

All new monies start with 0 users (maybe 1 if you want to be philosophical) and ultimately grow in network effect. Ultimately what decides what will become the money is the advantage and superiority that the money provides to its users over those who don't adopt it.

That within itself is the incentive for users of other monetary networks to adopt the most advantageous network.

Dollars are a good example of this, they are not actually "money".

They have almost no value (other than the paper it is printed on) however circulate through our economy as a medium of exchange based on our perception that someone beyond us will accept the paper that it is printed on.

That is the perceived value and thus why they are accepted.

When push comes to shove, Gold as an example will be far more accepted than worthless paper. As gold has utility and base value in Jewellery, electronics, and medicine whereas paper has base value in not much except for these origami or hats pictured below. Which to be fair, is pretty cool.

So those are the characteristics of sound money, now, let's think about it, where does money come from?

Money, when you think about it, is essentially the ultimate **proof of work.**

Money proves you have spent a finite resource (your time and/or resources) to produce something even more finite (generally gold, a commodity, product, good or service) that is of value to others... that is the key, you cannot have money without providing value to others through work.

That's the point of money.

A universal store of value, Medium of exchange and unit of account.

The important thing here to note is that in money, like anything else in this world, there is a limitation to it and that's what gives not only money, but everything it's value. In other words, the value of a money is derived from how hard it is to create more of the particular asset.

The pricing of goods in a market i.e., where something gets its value from, is simply based on the exchanging of goods produced.

In a theoretical sense, if a good that was easy to produce and had the same theoretical value as a good hard to produce then it would make sense to just produce the good that is easy to create and exchange it for the hard asset. Problem here though is that no one would end up producing the other good. Leading to a more severe shortage of the good that is hard to obtain. This is why price setting mechanisms, which we will inevitably see more of in the future from the government don't work, and secondly why anything of value has to inherently have a certain level of "hardness" about it.

Remember the concept, **proof of work**.

To provide value to others, there must be limitations to the ability to create that value.

What monies have we used in the past?

Examining monetary history will help us understand where we have come from and basically how we got to where we are today and then where we are moving to in the future. Additionally, what we should aim to create to achieve the most prosperity and equality of opportunity in society.

The money that has been chosen is generally what has both been available and what best represents the characteristics described earlier. There are some other interesting monetary concepts which we will go through as well.

At first, there was nothing...

There wasn't and still isn't a form of money that "just existed". So, the first forms of trade and money were just in the form of bartering and exchanging other non-fungible goods between vendors willing to sell a certain asset for another at arbitrary, non-uniform prices aka just people agreeing to trade goods based on perceived benefit i.e., a bushel of wheat for a chicken. That was the first semblance of money. Non-Fungible goods.

Whilst bartering initially worked for tens of thousands of years in early human development, at least to an extent. The solution could only ever go so far. As it was not scalable for a society where there are many different people with many different needs, situations, goals, and assets. Making it certainly not suitable for our global society today, nor any time within the past few thousand years.

There would inevitably come a time where we needed a universal money or something acting as a universal **store of value & medium of exchange** suitable to fit the needs of an ever growing and increasingly inter-connected species.

Beyond barter, many cultures around the world developed and adopted the use of a universal "commodity" as a money. Objects that, have utility value in themselves such as wheat or cows. This is what gave users confidence in value whilst being used as a money and later, having a monetary network that was backed by a commodity at a pegged value, aka collateralised money.

Circa 3000 BC, the Mesopotamian civilization developed a large-scale economy based on commodity money. The shekel was made of silver and was the unit of weight and currency, was equivalent to a specific weight of barley. Subconsciously implying that barley had more value than silver. Seems ludicrous today however it demonstrates that what is true today was even thousands of years ago, that value was and is subjective. Value is made up. Value doesn't exist. Value only exists in our heads.

The Babylonians and their neighbouring city states later developed the earliest known form of organised financial systems, in terms of rules on legal debt contracts and law codes relating to business practices and private property.

Point here being that money emerged and was adopted more extensively when the increasing benefits of a monetary system made it exponentially more useful to the network users.

This is a reason why gold has been extensively used as money for thousands of years. In this specific scenario of increasing financial complexity, the increased portability, divisibility and scarceness of gold vs other assets such as wheat, cows or even other metals, made it a very good money. Not only based on its own characteristic's vs other assets but its ability to easily be integrated into increasingly complex financial systems vs other assets, as we say with the gold florin, which we explore in more detail.

Moving down the monetary timeline, metals next, where available, were favoured for use as money over such commodities as cattle, cowry shells, or salt, because metals are more durable, portable, more divisible and you can even argue metals can provide greater utility than other commodities such as cattle, although the value of which is subjective. A significant milestone with metals being adopted as money was that 1kg of iron = 1kg of iron whereas previously 1 cow does not necessarily equal another cow. Cows, wheat, barley etc come in all sizes, shapes, conditions and qualities.

More abundant and widely known/distributed metals were adopted at first because in a totally isolated and not connected global/regional society, the need for recognition and usability was psychologically speaking, probably the most important drivers of adoption.

Bronze was one of the first universally recognised monies across Asia and Europe, often in the form of small knives and spades used in China during the Zhou dynasty circa 1000bc, with cast bronze replicas of cowrie shells in use before this.

Bronze cowrie shells

Evidence suggests that the first manufactured coins backed by their own metal commodity are thought to have appeared in India, China, and the cities around the Aegean Sea (modern day Greece/turkey) circa 7th century BC.

The technology of coinage was historically speaking, a big revolution as units of metals have predetermined/uniform values. This evolution in technology was an extra step up in fungibility from the previous versions of metal currencies.

The Aegean coins were stamped (heated and then hammered with some type of official insignia) whereas, the Indian coins from the Ganges River valley region were punched metal disks, and Chinese coins (first developed in the Great Plain) were cast bronze with holes in the centre to be strung together.

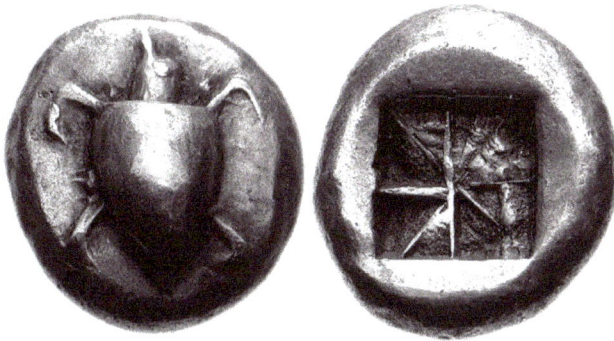

Very few Aegean coins still remain.

This is a Silver stater of Aegina, 550–530 BC

Ancient Chinese Bronze coins

The different forms and metallurgical processes imply a separate development of money based on what best served the needs of those adopting the currency.

The use of gold as a money has been traced back as far as the fourth millennium BC when the Egyptians used gold bars of a set weight as a medium of exchange, as had been done earlier in Mesopotamia with silver bars.

This was a step up from the other previously used precious metals used such as silver, bronze, copper, iron as gold from then on became the go to money and store of value around the world until essentially today as it was the apex predator in the money field due to its apex predator characteristics.

The adoption of gold as a money very much shaped the history of the world as we see it today. Every empire that grew adopted gold and conversely, every empire that did not adopt gold or debased the gold currency shrank/collapsed/ is in the process of collapsing.

The Achaemenid Persian empire grew on the back of using gold as a money when Cyrus the great introduced gold coin money. The strength of the empire would grow whilst gold coins were used by the empire.

The empire would end at the time they lost their gold, which was when Alexander the Great would invade, take the gold and remelt it into Greek money which also subsequently fuelled one of the largest empires of all time, spanning from Europe to India.

The Roman Empire was the first technologically advanced empire to build on a gold standard. The empire would only fall when the currency was becoming consistently debased over the course of centuries caused by increasing corruption and the unsustainable amounts of spending needed to fuel the empire.

Another system which facilitated empires to be build and more complex financial systems to form was the gold florin standard across Europe.

The Gold Florin was a coin made from pure 24-carat gold weighing 3.536 grams, minted in Florence in 1252.

The gold florin is commonly viewed to have been the first globally recognisable currency (at least between European nations and other trading nations) which was minted uniformly for a 280-year period between 1252 - 1533.

As many Florentine banks were also medieval multinational companies with branches across Europe, the florin quickly became the dominant trading money of Western Europe for large-scale transactions.

The gold florin also served as a strong base for the first multinational implementation of ledger technology. Since the base layer technology could be trusted, it served as a good base (at least for the period) to build financial complexity and functionality on top of it.

An important note to take is that the higher level of proof of work that was required for these monies was what drove the value to the users over long periods of time through the characteristics which we touched on before.

Those who didn't adopt the apex technology were disadvantaged, thus leaving them with no choice but to adopt the superior technology which in this case, was the technology of money.

With all this said, it's not so simple to say what was used and wasn't used for exact dates on a global level. Naturally, different resources were more abundant and scare in different areas, meaning that the money used in those global/universal societies depended on a huge variety of factors.

Some other strange and notable examples of money were as follows:

Shells.

Yes, Seashells.

Believe it or not, shells were used as money once upon a time. And believe it or not, they have been used quite extensively across the world by cultures and time periods unconnected to each other.

Shell money usually consisted of whole or partial sea shells, sometimes made into beads or simply left in its natural beauty.

The use of shells in money began as a direct exchange, in the same sense that we directly exchange cash for goods today. The shells were thought to have aesthetic and ornamental value. And after all, who doesn't like shiny things, right?

Side thought: In addition, to its utility, maybe this is partially why gold has value too? I suppose people inherently like shiny shells and by extension shiny rocks.

I'm not going to extensively cover the use of the shells across all cultures as it is mostly irrelevant to the purpose of the book but for the sake of good sportsmanship, I want to share a few.

The most valued shell by Native American tribes of the west coast was *Dentalium*, one of several species of tusk shell.

This shell money was valued by its length rather than simply the number of shells. The "ligua" was the highest denomination in their currency, which was around 6 inches long.

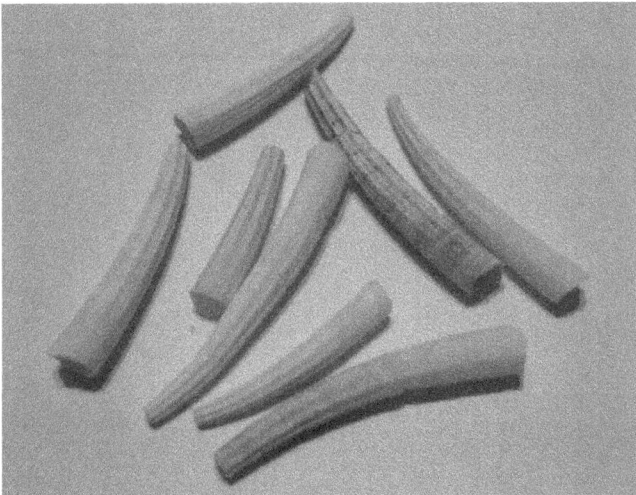

Pic by Ondasdomar - Own work, CC BY-SA 3.0,
https://commons.wikimedia.org/w/index.php?curid=24263724

On the western coast of Africa, shells were used as legal tender right up until the mid-19th century, just prior to the abolition of the slave trade.

The shells of the sparkling dwarf olive sea snail were harvested for use as currency in the Kingdom of Kongo. In fact, They have been known to be traded as far north as the Kingdom of Benin.

In China, cowry shells have also been so prominent in Chinese culture that many characters relating to money and trade contain the character for cowry: 貝. The first known use of cowry shells in China, dates back to over 3000 years ago.

In Orissa, India, cowry shells were used as currency right up until 1805 when it was abolished by the British East India Company and the Rupee aka Fiat money was enforced.

Cowry shells

And finally, In Australia, different types of shells were used by different tribes in the north, with one tribe's shell often being seen as worthless by another tribe.

Talk about fungibility problems that hindered trade and economic communication.

There are actually many more examples of shells being used as money however that's enough for now. Moving on.

Rai Stones (Giant stones)

Another example of odd forms of money were Rai Stones. These stones were crafted and treasured by the native inhabitants of the Yap islands in Micronesia as a form on money. They are also known as Yapese stone money.

Rai stones were typically crafted out of a crystalline limestone. The stone is a circular shape with a hole created in the centre. The smallest is approximately 3.5 centimetres in diameter whilst the largest remaining stone is 3.6 metres in diameter and 50 centimetres thick.

This is not the largest stone, but it certainly is the coolest looking one I could find.

Believe it or not, these stones were used as a form of money, and it worked as a public ledger system. Naturally, each stone had their perceived value based on how "hard" they were to create. Meaning the larger the stone, the more the value and after all, who would trade a large stone for a small stone when a small stone is much easier to create. Remember, proof of work.

The stones would sit in the middle of the village, outside meeting halls and honestly, just pretty well anywhere. The location of the stone wasn't necessarily overly important. The fact that it existed and had scarce value was seemingly enough to create a monetary system for them.

Instead of carting the stones around to pay for things like we would today with cash, the Rai stones were essentially just a public ledger system. The ownership of a stone would be transferred by declaring in front of the village about the transfer of ownership from the old owner to the new owner, thus the new owner was then able to store wealth and exchange their money for other goods in the future.

Salt

Considered so valuable that Roman Soldiers were sometimes paid with salt, instead of in their usual form being coins such as the siliqua discussed in this chapter. This is actually where the word for salary comes from, their monthly wage was called a "salarium" as "sal" was the Latin word for salt.

While these last few examples are cool to know. Again, notice. All money that ended up being successful was successful because there was the proof of work concept to it.

The very second money became too easy to acquire and too little work was required. The money lost a tremendous amount of its scarcity/value and became worthless leading to the demise of the users of the monetary network an often the empires that were propped up because of the currency... as we saw with Shells, Rai stones and to be fair, nearly every other type of money used up until this point except for gold and largely silver too.

To expand on this a bit further and to show you a few examples of how rises and falls have played out time and time again, let's have a look at some of the fiat currencies, which are the worst types of money known to man

.

"Fiat" for those unaware, means "by decree". It is money by decree. Meaning that the money only exists because someone (usually being a state, regime or monarchy) says so and has the physical prowess to enforce it. The money was not chosen by the free market and cannot survive without guns & threats to enforce its use, although it may not seem like it to those who are just average joe users of fiat money.

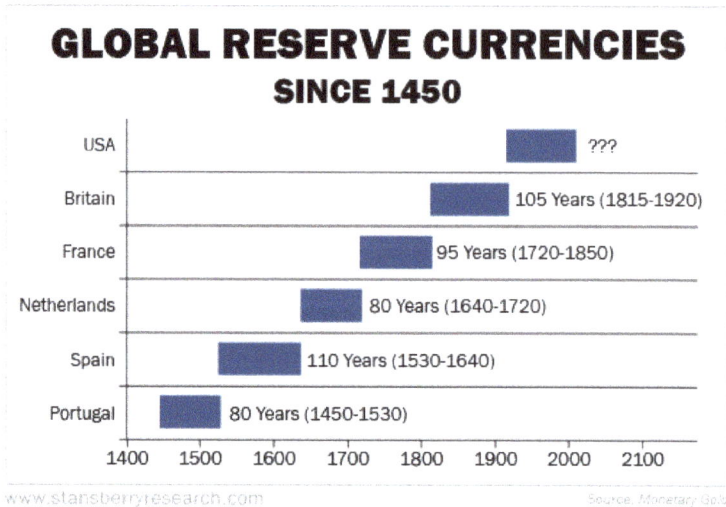

GLOBAL RESERVE CURRENCIES SINCE 1450

USA ???
Britain 105 Years (1815-1920)
France 95 Years (1720-1850)
Netherlands 80 Years (1640-1720)
Spain 110 Years (1530-1640)
Portugal 80 Years (1450-1530)

www.stansberryresearch.com   Source: Monetary Gold

I will not go into the extensive history of each empire and what led to the ability to enforce these currencies as the global reserve, the exacts of the empires and what led to the demise of each empire etc as this is not a dedicated book on the history of empires and writing this could take 1000 pages within itself, thus I feel it would detract from the readability and to be fair, the purpose of the book.

For a detailed history and analysis of this subject, I highly recommend Ray Dalio's "A changing world order".

But as Elvis would say "it goes a little something like this".

The stages on an empire are usually as follows:

1) Peace and prosperity following a change in the power structure.
2) Financial bubble and wealth gap
3) Economic bust and economic downturn
4) Printing Money & Credit

5) Revolution & Wars
6) Debt & Restructuring

From a monetary point of view, the currencies seen as the reserve currencies of the world, at least initially, had some kind of real value. You need to remember that as I mentioned, money doesn't "just exist".

People from all over the world have a vast array of different needs, goals, ambitions etc and even ways of thinking. Thus, needed as they still do need, a trusted medium of exchange to break down these barriers as a means of transferring value even across time, space and even cultures.

These currencies were initially made from or backed by real assets of value (usually metals) HOWEVER over time, became diluted and debased for many different reasons, for example, a lack of ability of the empire to pay their bills i.e., when the Romans "coin clipped" the denarius as they couldn't afford to support an ever growing empire and war chest associated with a large expansive empire with many enemies on many fronts becoming increasingly hostile, sensing the weakness.

A clipped siliqua

An unclipped siliqua

A note to take from this last part of the chapter about reserve currencies is that, again, the money survived as long as it had value.

When debasement of the money happened, essentially when the value came "by decree", that was inevitably the start of the end for the currency and for the empire which it supported.

Similarly, when the apex money was adopted and those left "holding the bags" of the money that was no longer the most desirable good were subsequently demonetized. As we saw with China in the 1800's when they remained on a silver standard whilst the western world was moving to a gold standard. Because of this, China lost much power in this period, and it wasn't until the cultural revolution (1966 – 1976) that China started to fulfil its role as a major global playing. Fulfilling Napoleon Bonaparte's prediction, "Let China Sleep, for when she wakes, she will shake the world".

The succeeding money adopted beyond the failing currencies provided more value to the network of users. The succeeding money was always adopted due to it better suiting the characteristics of money.

The most apex money always won and those with the most apex money always sustained period of prosperity and success whilst they maintained real hard money. Extrapolating that fact forward, the most apex money will continue to win out over a long enough period and those with the most apex money will also continue to have the most prosperity.

Fiat always has and always will die. A collapse is, gradually, then suddenly.

This is a perfect segue into the next chapter.

Chapter 2

The Fiat Ponzi

Often when I am explaining Monero or even just crypto in general to people, I say to understand the point of Monero, Bitcoin and crypto, you actually need to understand many other areas of knowledge first and at minimum, have a moderate level understanding in those areas.

Those areas of understanding include history, money, finance, technology, politics and game theory, just to name a few.

Generally, these topics take tens of thousands of hours of study to understand them on a meaningful level. Knowledge or therefore, a lack of, is probably one of the largest factors as to why society accepts fiat money today, even after thousands of years and countless attempt of failed fiat money.

Simply telling people about Bitcoin or Monero or whatever coin doesn't mean anything unless you understand the purpose of it, from a zoomed out point of view and can also understand on a more than superficial level what problems it can actually fix. Which inevitably leads to the question from them about what the problems actually are.

You may have been stuck with an aunty/ uncle, normie family member or general normie at one stage trying to explain "crypto" to them in a simple way and truth be told, There really just is no simple way without going on a 2 hour tangent that leaves everyone asleep, ready to kill themselves or worse and I'm sure you know this feeling, when they stare blindly at you like you are a crazy conspiracy theorist.

Any true Monero militant, Bitcoin maximalist or hard money maximalist in general has surely been through this at one stage.

Because the reality is that the monetary and global financial systems are purposely designed to be clear as mud, hard to understand (with an added layer of complex jargon thrown on top to really confuse and mislead everyone).

These systems are also purposely designed to be opaque so no one can easily "see in" to discover the truth of the system and how these systems really work. Which includes all the shady dealings between elites, globalists and central bankers that secure the fiat systems place in society, but we will touch on that specific topic later in the book.

The truth of it all, is so far away from the propagated societal narratives and norms, that daring to explain it makes you look crazy. Though, some may call that "the perfect plan".

So, when you try to explain step 1 of Monero/Bitcoin to your normie family, you also need to explain the entire complex global monetary and financial systems… just as one topic. Which is sure to lose everyone and have them looking at you like you are a conspiracy theorist. A feeling I know all too well.

It's through this opaqueness and distorted "truths" that the fiat monetary system and the shills who support it are able to thrive. As it keeps the everyday person completely unaware and completely disinterested in how they are getting stolen from and manipulated every single day of their lives.

So, I have tried to boil it down as simply as possible here, so that you can have a simple way of explaining it all, or better, so that a person who is unfamiliar with it all can read this and still understand it.

The chapter is quite detailed and remember, it is incredibly important to understand these concepts to truly understand the underlying problems that hard, sound, decentralised and "unfuckable" money fixes.

There have been a few attempts at paper money throughout history however for the sake of the relevance, we will stick mainly to the 20th century as we briefly covered the history of money already and it tells us directly how we got to the Ponzi like fiat monetary system that we have today. Sticking to the current fiat Ponzi also allows us to understand what is happening TODAY!

To those unaware, paper currency was created as a "debt instrument", essentially just a tool to represent specific weights of precious metals being gold and silver, held at depository institutes such as banks. The gold and silver were originally redeemable by the holder of the "paper receipt" for that specific weight of gold or silver.

The bills were simply a receipt for gold and silver, tradeable for any purchases as it easier to carry paper than precious metals, not to mention easier to divide too.

Below are some examples of gold and silver certificates.

$1 Silver Certificate

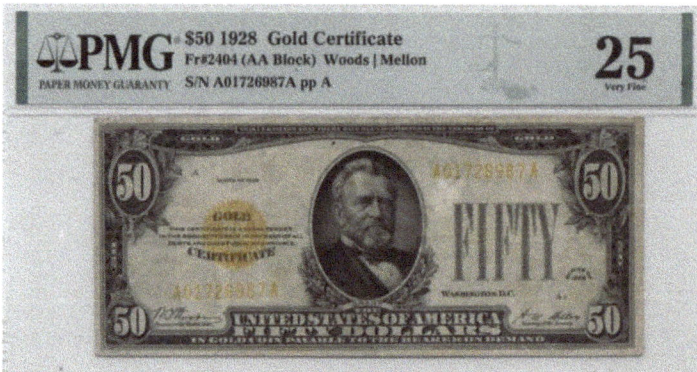

$50 Gold Certificate

You may have glanced past the subtle difference at first between these notes and the notes we see today. However, as you can see above, it states that the note is "payable to the bearer", the amount of the specific metal (gold or silver) in dollar value previously deposited at an institution.

Essentially, as mentioned, what was created was just an easily exchangeable system between paper money and what was seen as real money (gold)... This, in short is known as the gold standard.

The history of paper money initially started as a good idea.

The money itself wasn't able to be printed out of thin air like we see today. The only way to create cash was to trade a valuable finite resource (gold or silver) for these notes. Thus, being the natural limitation of its creation.

So, when gold or silver was handed into the depository, the cash would be "minted" and on the other side when the gold or silver was redeemed, the cash would be made obsolete and taken out of circulation. Essentially "burned", as a term that is used in crypto today.

What kept the bank depositories honest (at least theoretically, them not being able to print money out of thin air) was the fact that the cash was redeemable for real world assets in gold and silver and to over hypothecate these assets would lead to liabilities on the bank as they were directly redeemable, thus the bank would have to supply the gold and silver in some way, shape or form.

If the bank was to over hypothecate and not be able to meet their liabilities, the depository would become bankrupt if there was to be a run on the bank, leading to the end of poor practices and also leads to the incentive to not engage in these practices in the first place. In addition, those responsible would go to jail... simple concept, right? This was a combination of both natural (going broke) and manmade (going to jail) incentive structures that kept money scarce and thus valuable. Although going broke alone is enough of a free market incentive that has proved to work over and over again throughout history.

It is the exact same incentive structure that has been used on Sam Bankman-Fried and his over hypothecation of assets through the FTX exchange. The market speaks when it comes to poor practices.

This is why cash is called a "debt instrument", because the cash implied that the holder of the gold/silver i.e., "the bank" owed "the bearer" i.e., the person holding the cash, the amount i.e., "the sum" of what was seen as the real money, which was gold and silver.

Gold and silver are all limited/finite and non-replicable/fakable resources. It is either gold or silver or it's not. There is no middle ground. You cannot chemically fake gold and/or silver. And despite all the efforts over the centuries, you cannot create gold and silver by any process other than mining the naturally occurring precious metals.

Again, the important distinction in this process is that the only way to obtain gold and silver besides mining of course was to provide value to someone else. Which, like mining, as a concept, is limited by labour and resources. There are only so many hours in the day and only so many things you can do in those hours... Importantly too, competing with others to provide value.

The obtaining of gold and silver thus was limited. Meaning, the scarcity to obtain it, was also what gave it value. There was the limitation. Scarcity in money seems obvious quality to have however as we will discuss, that is far from how money is created today with no limiting factors. There is almost no scarcity, which ultimately makes it worthless or worth only the object that it is, being paper. This will show on a long enough time period. devaluation is a process, not an event.

That was the limiting factor to it all and ultimately what gave money it's value.

This, however, was to change.

Following the Panic of 1907, where the stock market fell over 50% over a matter of 3 weeks, the Federal reserve was introduced in 1913 through the Federal Reserve Act. To give some context of the panic, and to help understand the attitudes of the day, the panic of 1907 was triggered by a failed attempt of major banks to corner the market on the United Copper Company Stock.

When the attempt failed, banks that had lent money to the cornering scheme suffered runs from depositors that later spread to affiliated banks, meaning that the people and business' that had savings accounts with the banks were withdrawing their cash due to fears that the banks were insolvent and didn't have enough money to meet the demands of all deposits. It was due to these runs on the banks that lead to a significant decrease in the overall liquidity within the economy for institutional investors to use which ultimately caused the economy to retract. Simple maths.

Essentially, given that these banks and financial institutions play such a large role in loans & investments etc, the knock-on effects in regards to spending and growth were severely damaged.

In the end, it was due to the famous banker that we all know today, J.P Morgan, who invested his money and convinced other bankers increase liquidity available in the economy, that led to the resurgence of confidence in the economy, spending, growth etc.

I do want to point out here, that this is a case in point of how free markets find a solution that doesn't involve stealing purchasing power from others... Anyway, continuing.

As mentioned earlier, in 1913, The government headed by Woodrow Wilson introduced the Federal Reserve Act, thereby establishing the Federal reserve, having gained a majority in the House of representatives and senate the year before in 1912.

The panic of 1907 was used to justify the need for the federal reserve bank to give government the ability to avoid panics and recessions of this nature. The idea was that the federal reserve could pump money into the system when required to avoid this type of crises in the future.

The Federal Reserve Act created twelve different regional Federal Reserve Banks jointly responsible for managing the country's monetary supply, making loans and providing oversight to banks. Additionally, they essentially served as a lender of last resort, always available to create money to be distributed when seen fit by the small elite group of bankers, of course "in the national interest".

I don't know for a matter of fact about whether or not this was broadly believed by the public, but you can see, at minimum, why this lip service was enough to get the public to accept it. It is most likely that the general public didn't understand the consequences of making the decision thus allowed the creation of the fed in order to make their current pain go away.

This is just another example of how fear and literal panic in this case, was used to take control of what surmounts to rights, freedoms, and the strength of the population.

The President who over saw the creation of the Federal Reserve also knew the beast which he created.

In Woodrow Wilsons book titled "Woodrow Wilson: The New Freedom", he wrote "However it has come about, it is more important still that the control of credit also has become dangerously centralized. It is the mere truth to say that the financial resources of the country are not at the command of those who do not submit to the direction and domination of small groups of capitalists who wish to keep the economic development of the country under their own eye and guidance. The great monopoly of this country is the monopoly of big credits. So long as that exists, our old variety of freedom and individual energy of development are out of the question. A great industrial nation is controlled by its system of credit. Our system of credit is privately concentrated."

This is what makes me believe that his intention for creating the Federal Reserve was not a malicious one, it was in fact an intention coming from a good place.

In any case, this, ladies and gentlemen, is what led to the creation of the Federal Reserve.

This believe or not, the creation of "the fed" as it's come to be known as, was only the beginning of the Ponzi. The true evil of the Ponzi was still to come.

In 1934, The USA performed their first heist of gold. A heist that was only a taste of things to come, in terms of magnitude.

The Gold Reserve Act of 1934 was the first divorce between gold and the monetary system that was backed by it. No private household, bank, or business was allowed to own or hold more than a very small amount of gold. Gold coins were forbidden for monetary purposes.

More maliciously, This Act also authorized the president, Franklin Roosevelt, to raise the price of gold by 60 percent.

Treasury gold stock, valued at $4,033 million in January 1934, became $7,348 million in February 1934, an increase of $3,405 million by the decree of one man.

On the other side of this "increase", the average person now needed more of these promissory notes to redeem the same amount of gold, thus stealing 37.5% of the people's gold. But since gold was essentially illegal to own, what did it matter, right?

Not a bad plan

Next major event on the path to the fiat Ponzi was WW2, Initially the US stayed neutral and supplied both sides of the war with all materials necessary for a war. This meant that the US was able to accrue large amount of Europe's gold by selling armaments, equipment, food, industrial materials etc to the warring factions in Europe. It was only later that the US joined the war.

Due to the fact that they sold to the warring factions before they joined the fighting and subsequently seized large amounts of gold from the Germans, Italians etc whilst they were involved in the fighting. Ultimately, they were able to hold a large amount of the world gold.

By the end of the war, the US held 90% of the world's gold at the time. A huge portion.

As the end of the war neared, the allies and nations of the world came together in 1944 to a United Nations conference called the Bretton-woods conference that was held between July 1 to 22.

The agreement that was signed, expanded the dollar system to the post-WWII world. A system where the dollar was made the reserve currency of the world which was backed by gold at a fixed rate of $35 USD per oz of Gold. By extension foreign currencies would then be tied the US dollar at fixed rates.

I.e. "£0.24 GBP = $1 USD"

         &

 "$35 USD = 1oz Gold"

The idea was that since the US dollar was now convertible by nations to gold i.e. The US dollar was a paper claim to gold, this is what would keep the US honest since as if they over printed then the nations could redeem the gold and the US would then have no gold and be broke, hence the incentive to be honest and not overprint US dollars. This was giving the US the inch for the mile they will come to take in the future.

To be fair, in theory, the idea was not necessarily too bad of an idea as the world had just gone through 2 world wars in a relatively short period of time and was in dire need of more international cooperation following not only 2 world wars but also colonial empire wars that had been going on for the previous 500 - 1000 years.

The theory was that having a unified global monetary instrument such as this would make it far easier to achieve global economic co-operation as there were less barriers to entry, less confusing regulation and less burdensome procedures to follow as well as theoretically making international bullying harder via exclusion. Since the currencies themselves were backed by an asset of real value and scarcity, being gold, there was supposedly real value behind the paper notes.

Specifically, The Bretton Woods system required countries to guarantee the convertibility of their currencies into U.S. dollars on demand within 1% of the fixed parity rates outlined in the agreement, with the dollar ultimately being convertible to gold bullion for foreign governments and central banks at US$35 per troy ounce of fine gold (or 0.88867 gram fine gold per dollar).

To be fair though, considering the US held 90% of the known gold supply, there was little room for negotiation from other countries, and so they were essentially forced into agreeing to the new system or risk being left out of the global economy all together.

I think it's important to note that unlike the pre-WWII period. The convertibility of dollars into gold was not available to average joe, even the average joes of the USA. This convertibility system of dollars to gold was only open to other central banks and foreign governments of the world.

The Agreements that were signed also established the International Bank for Reconstruction and Development (IBRD), which later became part of the World Bank and also established the International Monetary Fund (IMF). This led to what was called the Bretton Woods system for international commercial and financial relations.

Since the US had avoided the destruction of its country whilst Europe had been destroyed in large parts, due to a historically unseen amount of broad level destruction, it meant that the US was able to further leverage the need of Europe and loan out the gold as Europe needed to be rebuilt.

This system of universal convertibility of dollars to gold worked (at least, for what it was worth) for a period of time. Unlike the economic growth of today, we saw real economic growth during this post war period and an increase in the standard of living brought about by increased innovation and increased productivity of valuable goods and services (real economic output).

We could add a conspiracy about JFK in here to further the belief of Woodrow Wilson that the fed and group of elite bankers had gained tremendous power, but we won't for the sake of the book.

The system of gold backed convertible money was halted all together in 1971.

During the proceeding decades, an increasingly "fat" US government was amounting an ever increasing amount of debt due to events such as The Vietnam War & The Cold War (along with other increased non-productive consumption based spending). To combat this, the US government decided to over hypothecate the amount of bills in circulation vs the amount of gold in reserves using a variety of debt related methods (the details of which are probably too confusing for the purpose of the book).

Essentially, given the limited amount of gold that the US Treasury held, or at least claimed to hold, versus the larger amount of gold claims in the hands of 'foreign' central banks all over the world, this naturally caused panic in the US government and the US Treasury that the remaining US gold stockpile would be 'drained' by foreign central banks converting their huge US dollar balances into gold at the US Treasury gold window.

It was becoming increasingly obvious to holders of the dollar around the world, that there were not enough assets (gold) to cover the amount of debt (paper notes). So, like in 1907 when ,the banks received a run from depositors, the same thing happened to the depositories that held the gold. It essentially became a race to see who was the last one holding the would be worthless paper notes.

Secretary of Treasury John Connally is quoted on tape as saying, "In the international field the problem is one, the convertibility of dollars into gold and we're going to have to stop that at some point...Everybody, I say 'everybody', most people tend to think that ten billion dollars (in gold reserves) is the point below which we should not go."

Later in the conversation, Nixon and Connally were joined by White House Chief of Staff H.R Haldeman. Connally and Haldeman speak about just how serious the gold drain has become and the ramifications for the US. Haldeman notes that the United States has lost $850 million in gold reserves in the week of August 2, 1971, alone.

Connally explains that the French have also called in over $1 billion in reserves in the past few weeks and that the Germans and the Dutch are looking to call in some $200-250 million more. Connally thinks that the President could hold on to a decision until mid-September, but not later.

Subsequently, a drastic & world altering event took place.

On August 15, 1971, President and resident thief Richard Nixon stood Infront of the nation and decided the best way forward out of the ever surmounting debt accrued mainly from unproductive, consumption based spending was to deceive quite literally the entire world and justify the theft of their gold.

His speech is as follows *" I have directed Secretary Connally to suspend temporarily the convertibility of the dollar into gold or other reserve assets, except in amounts and conditions determined to be in the interest of monetary stability and in the best interests of the United States."*

I'll give you a hint here, what Richard Nixon actually meant was that the United States was unable to meet its obligations to other countries i.e., it didn't have enough gold to pay its mounting debts from decades of wars being Vietnam, Korea and a subtle "cold war" of subversion against the Soviet Union.

What this meant at the end of the day, was that they performed the greatest heist in the history of the world by keeping and not making redeemable the gold that we the people trusted and previously converted into IOU notes that were cash "gold and silver deposit certificates".

Since the paper notes were no longer convertible into Gold & silver, as previously promised, this was the creation of money by decree. Money now got its value by decree. Which is what? That's right, Fiat money

Fiat = by decree

They decommissioned the debt instruments and issued paper notes that are quite literally only worth the paper they're printed on (they do look pretty cool though). They took the gold and silver then gave paper to the people... literally. Not redeemable for gold and silver anymore.

A big lol at the public from the reserve bankers.

Zooming out, we can see that:

1) At first, Gold was money.
2) Then paper was money backed by gold which could be redeemed by everyone.
3) Then it was only redeemable by central banks & foreign governments.
4) Then redeemable by nobody.

A classic case of the frog boiling in the pot.

If anyone else did this previously, they would have gone to jail for the rest on eternity. In fact, there was someone very famous who ran a very large Ponzi scheme, I'm sure you know him. His name is Bernie Madoff, he did something very similar and was sentenced to 150 years in jail and subsequently died in jail in 2021.

He, like the US government took deposits, deceived his depositors and then became insoluble, meaning that he was unable to pay to his depositors what he owed them, meaning that he stole from his client/depositors.

Exact same here, except the people who did it in the case of the US government were perhaps too powerful to ever face any responsibility for it.

In fact, Richard Nixon received a state funeral as all presidents do. However, when you zoom out and think about it, the fact that the mastermind of the largest heist in history received a state funeral, is quite staggering but rather typical of history I suppose.

The de-pegging of the dollar from gold and silver enabled what has become a continued theft of people's wealth over the past 51 years since 1971 through debasement/inflation caused by the printing of money that has been an addiction of governments till this day and has become synonymous with monetary policy.

Let's, have a look how this was caused.

Basic economics tells us that supply vs demand are the 2 factors that decide the price of any good/ service or asset.

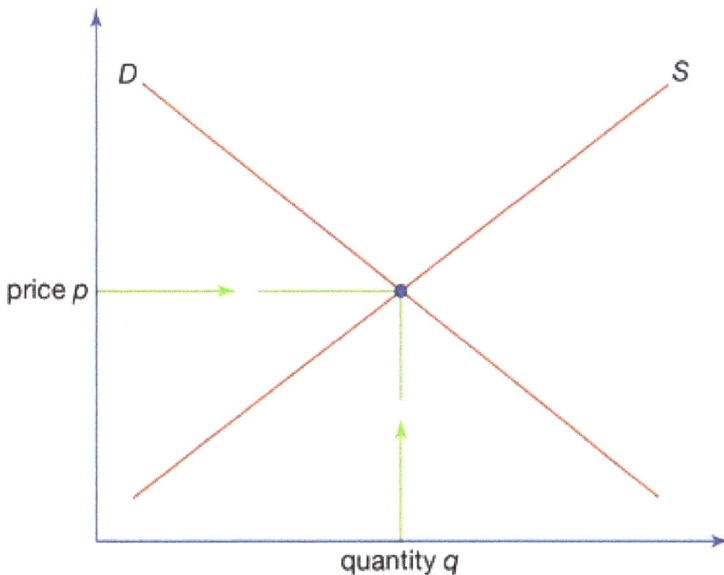

The price of an asset is determined where the supply curve of an asset meets the demand curve for an asset. Basic Economics.

So, what they have done since 1971 is increase the supply... quite significantly and artificially.

Without increasing demand for it through productivity or as in the past, gold to back it up. In fact, the 685 billion in circulation in 1971 wasn't backed by anything so that within itself was a Ponzi.

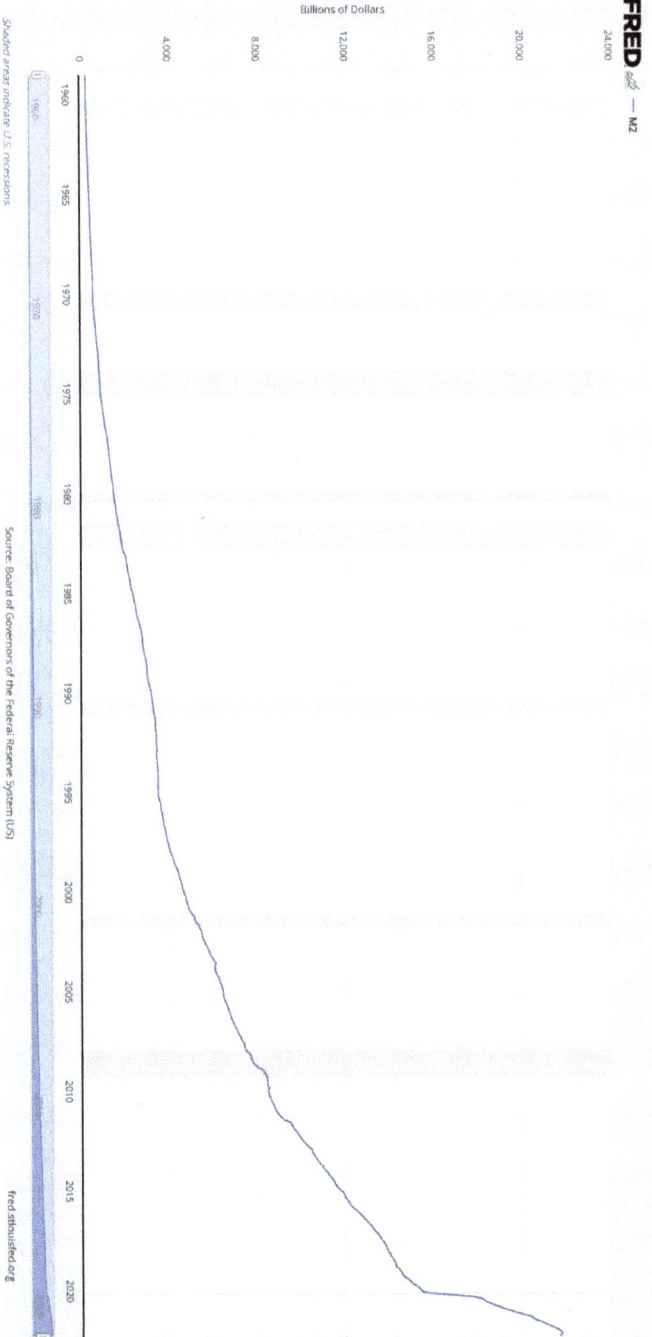

FRED — M2

Billions of Dollars

Shaded areas indicate U.S. recessions.

Source: Board of Governors of the Federal Reserve System (US)

fred.stlouisfed.org

Between 1971 to today (2022), The M2 supply which measures the amount of cash, checking deposits, and easily-convertible near money*, rose from $685 Billion to $22 Trillion... and increase of over 3200%.

*For clarity, *"easily convertible near money"* is savings accounts, certificates of deposit (CDs), foreign currencies, money market accounts, marketable securities, and Treasury bills

3211.67% to be precise. With the supply of dollars in circulation increasing every day. That's over 32x the original supply.

Meaning you need $32 today for every $1 you had in 1971 to not lose purchasing power based on the volume of the monetary supply. Even seasoned investors can struggle to achieve those types of returns. Certainly, saving into a bank account make this completely impossible.

So, let's now go back to our supply vs demand chart and let's map out what an increase in supply vs same amount of demand looks like

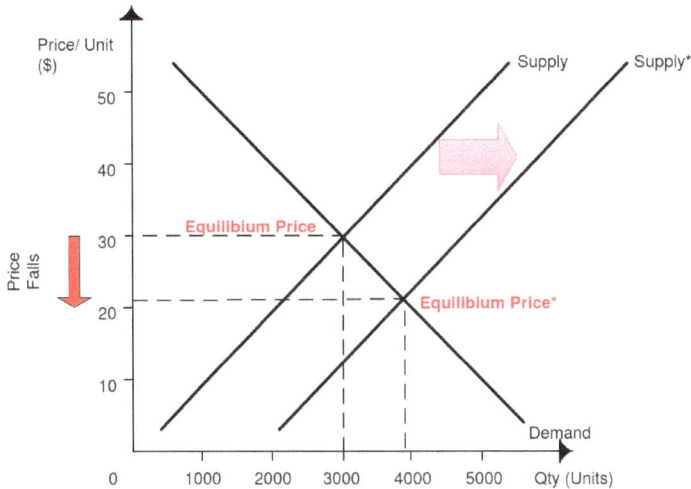

Impact of Increase in Supply with no change in Demand

As you can see, when we move the supply curve (increase supply), the value of that asset goes down. This is without even mapping a decrease in demand because after all, it is backed up by thin air. There is no new demand via productivity or gold to meet the new amount of money.

This is how when the government prints money via loans from the federal reserve and other lending facilities to "stimulate the economy", they are not making anyone richer, they are not helping anyone at all, they are simply making the current holders of the dollar poorer i.e., you and I, and just giving that purchasing power to themselves. I.e., taking from the holders and giving to the printers.

If you potentially think that this proportionately takes from both the rich and the poor equally then you are severely mistaken. Wealthy people don't hold their wealth in cash/dollars. They hold it in real assets like precious metals, stocks, cryptocurrencies etc. Whereas the low – middle class of society are the ones who hold a majority of the cash and also a much larger % of their net worth in cash in comparison to the wealthy.

Meaning that the lower – middle class of society is the one taking the biggest hit to their purchasing power and are carrying the biggest burden when the government implements policies that allow the printing of money out of thin air "in their best interest".

Additionally, the spending of the money created, almost always goes to the companies who produce real goods or services. The ownership of these company stocks, are generally by wealthy people, so this in turn also makes the rich richer via increased dividends and increased valuations of the companies that are producing the goods which are being sold, whilst making the poor poorer... but still, lets blame the "greedy capitalists", right?

Still think politicians and government stimuluses are able to help the everyday person.

Still think stimulus cheques help you "deal with the rising cost of living" or whatever other garbage they spiel to get you to buy it, are in your best interest?

All you have is the degradation of your current purchasing power. Now there is only more money, fighting for the same amount of goods in a shorter period of time, which equals inflation, which equals further degradation of your purchasing power, which equals you being poorer every single second they do this.

Print Money >>> Prices Go Up >>> Need More Money >>> Print Money >>> Prices Go Up >>> Need More Money >>> Print More Money... It's a vicious cycle that can only end one way.

This is why when people support policies such as "free this" or "free that", I am dumbfounded. As these policies can only be propped up by printing of money, which again, makes you poorer, because the lower – middle classes are actually paying for it more than anyone else including the politicians who made up these narratives for their own selfish personal gain (or perhaps it is well intentioned, in which case I don't know whether ignorance or malice is a better excuse)

They believe it is actually helping them when in fact it is harming them the most.

Basic maths.

Anyway, back on topic.

So, why do people and nations put up with this? Why isn't the money just worth nothing?

Here's where it may get slightly complicated so bear with me and read over it many times if you need, there is no shame in that.

Part of the reason is that the creation of dollars is actually supported by the "demand" created for them by the federal reserve who "loan" money printed out of fresh air to the government, then on their balance sheets as an asset that in theory will be paid back. In essence, they print in (increase supply) then ask for it back + plus interest (Increase demand)

Got your head around that?

Good, so let's move onto the maths of it.

Each debt based asset that has value must be met with a liability i.e., a supply must have a demand for it to be valuable. As we saw with cash on the gold standard. The asset (cash) was met by a liability (gold). And since people wanted gold, that was where the value came from. Meaning if you had the asset of cash, somebody had the liability to provide you with gold.

Assets – Liability = 0 = no devaluation = stable pricing

So, when the federal reserve creates an "asset" (cash) out of thin air, it is met by the liability of the government to pay it back. Plus, interest (which is a Ponzi within itself) but that's another topic.

The federal reserve provides liquidity to the government in the form of loans, from which they create the money out of thin air.

Another method used to put money into the system is via increasing the reserves available to banks via the federal reserve and since the banking system is what is called "fractional reserve" which means that the banks only need to hold a fraction of the money they loan out as actual cash on their balance sheets, it means that they are able the increase the amount available for loans to business' and people like you and I when they increase the reserves available to banks.

Both these methods require an asset being cash via a loan and a debt being the promise to pay it back.

Thus, Assets – liabilities = 0 … technically

Whereas, if it were just blatant printing out of thin air then it would lead to severe devaluation, very quickly. Not a bad trick, hey?

Side note: The federal reserve is supposed to be independent of the government however in reality, they are absolutely not. We see this via the appointment of the fed chairman via the president and subsequently the fed chairman implementing monetary policy that is always coincidently in favour of the president political agendas.

The consequence of this system becomes that the federal reserve is FORCED to buy these bonds "in the interest of economic stability". That means they are the buyer of last resort when no one else will prop up the Ponzi. This is not a free market where people/corporations are voluntarily lending their money to the government, because if it was, they government would have run out of buyers by now as they would not have been able to meet their obligations. Thus the people who lent them money would have lost it, which provides the incentive for the market not to make bad decisions in lending money to governments (or anyone for that matter) that can't pay it back.

The only other alternative to not become bankrupt/insolvent is to be more efficient with the debt that government takes on board, they would have had to spend it on productive assets that increase productivity which is ultimately economic prosperity. Not the consumption based spending that they waste it on at the moment, that benefits very very very few people. (Military industrial complex, Big Pharma, subsidies for big oil... etc etc etc)

I bet you also didn't know that many organisations like pension funds for example are mandated to buy government bonds and put them on their books. Further artificially increasing demand within the Ponzi.

When you take out all the artificial demand legislated by the government, there is really very few people willing to lend money to the government . As we see right now, hence why the government needs the fed to step in to buy the bonds in the first place... End side note.

With all this said, there is still devaluation of the dollar though, just based on the shear amount of dollars fighting over what is the same amount of good and services (adjusted for technological advances)

That's all inflation is caused by when you think about it, an increased amount of dollars fighting over the same amount of good and services available on the market, in too short a period of time.

The other reason that dollars still have value is simply because people accept them, obviously value is subjective and the fact that people accept them in with the faith they will be able to pass them onto someone else, is the other part of the reason as to why they still have some have value despite actually only being worth the paper they're printed on.

With that said, what gets people to accept them in the first place is the hegemony that enforces the use of paper money and the "brainwashing" of the population, for a lack of a better word. As populations, broadly speaking, don't understand what money actually is and every reference to money in all cultural norms is referred to as paper money, it's really all people know.

In regard to inflation, they are doing well to get away with it.

How well are they doing?

Well, let's look at it.

Let's look at devaluation of purchasing power vs the increase in monetary supply and come up with a beta number (A number that tells us how that asset acts compared to all other assets) to represent how much the increase of the monetary supply has outperformed the increase of prices... or vice versa.

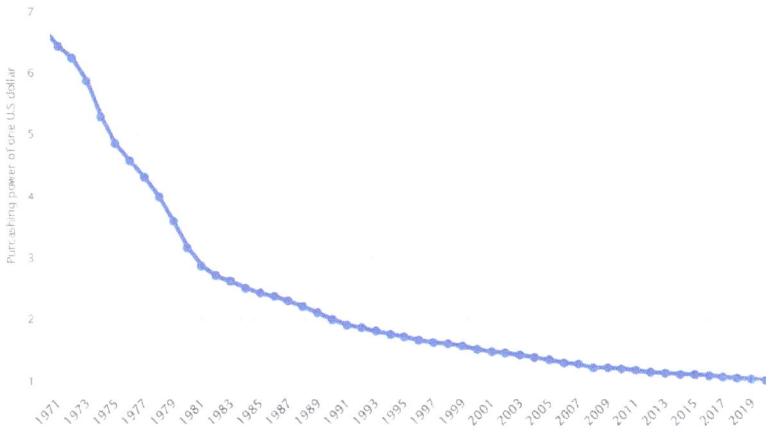

The chart above shows that we had 6.43x more purchasing power in 1971 vs today for 1 dollar according to statista.com.

Meaning $1 today was worth $6.43 in 1971 in a purchasing power sense.

This means the dollar has lost 84.44% of its purchasing power vs real assets in 51 years.

In other words, you would need $6.43 dollars today to purchase what you could purchase for $1 back in 1971... not exactly a great savings technology.

The only reason you need $6.43 today vs 1971 is because of the artificial creation of money and the lack of work required to create more dollars.

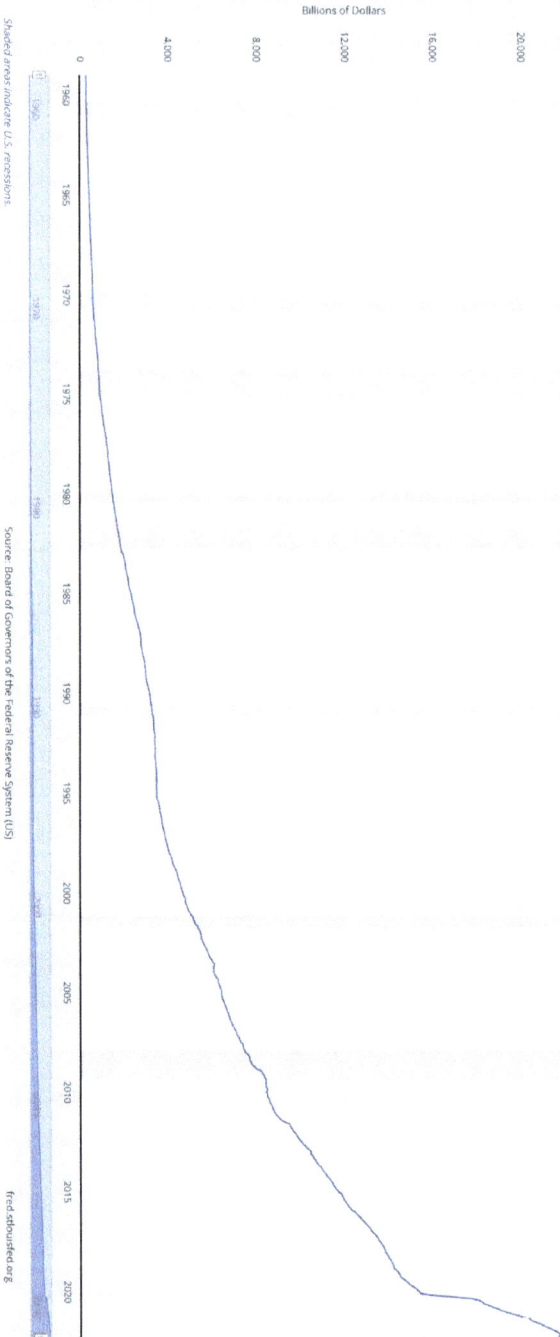

FRED — M2

Billions of Dollars

24,000

20,000

16,000

12,000

8,000

4,000

0

1960 1965 1970 1975 1980 1985 1990 1995 2000 2005 2010 2015 2020

Shaded areas indicate U.S. recessions.

Source: Board of Governors of the Federal Reserve System (US)

fred.stlouisfed.org

As we discussed earlier, the increase in supply has been 3211.67%

Which is 32.11x more money in the economy from 1971 until now (May 2022)

So, to calculate the beta we need to divide the increase in supply / Decrease in purchasing power.

Beta = 32.11 / 6.43 = 4.993

This means that the the increase of the monetary supply has outperformed the increase of prices.

by a factor of 4.993

Not bad, I'd be happy with that If I were the fed.

That is after all, essentially free purchasing power/money for the government and some individuals at the expense of everyone else.

But Michael, you said this was a Ponzi? Ponzi's all end and this sounds sustainable, right?

Well, this brings us to how it plays out and ultimately ends.

Remember, history shows us that systems are only functioning if people are enforcing them and that anything only has value if people perceive them to have value.

This system of the fiat money and by extension, the US dollar. Relies solely on enforcement and US hegemony from the status of the US dollar as the reserve currency of the world (introduced after WW2 with the Bretton woods system) but when you boil it down, it relies solely on enforcement which is just physical force at the end of the day.

There is no inherent value backing up this money anymore. It lost that when they de-pegged from the gold standard.

cough Which is why they have invaded every country that tried to create a different monetary system. Libya and Iraq. Coincidence? And that the countries who are "enemies" of the west being North Korea, Iran, Somalia, Syria are the only countries without central banks. Coincidence? I'll leave that for you to decide. Let's stick to maths.

We need to look at game theory here for a second. You need to remember that over a long enough period of time, people use the monetary system/network that brings them the most value.

If you are constantly being debased (losing value) vs a user of a network where they are not being debased (in essence, gaining more value from the use of that monetary network), people will switch the better monetary system over a long enough period of time through a natural incentive structure, it is a process, not an event. We have 4000 years of monetary history to back that up. That much is indisputable.

Not only in money, but people too, almost always take the most palatable approach/ path of least resistance. Sure, this can be manipulated for a while but since this process happens over a given period of time, each event taking place in that period of time will skew the probabilities of a particular outcome in a given direction. I.e.,

- Being debased 10% incentivises a certain % of people to look for alternatives.

- Being debased 20% incentivises a certain % of people to look for alternatives.

So on and so forth.

The evidence is clear, with the adoption of cryptocurrencies as a savings technology alone. Not to mention the cultural norms of gold being a store of value. The stronger the debasing becomes, the more incentives people have to look for alternatives. Thus, an event (debasement) skews probabilistic outcomes for a different event to happen (alternatives).

I think that currently, the acceptability/network effect of dollars vs other monies (not to mention they shut down attempted competitors such as E-gold) is what keeps the dollar used today.

Everyone accepts dollars, so to move to another monetary network provides exponentially less value to the adopter than to simply use the monetary network that everyone else already uses.

Even without the physical enforcement of the hegemony, this is why adoption of new monetary networks (or technology in general, as money is just a technology) can be rather slow. Slowly then suddenly.

Mobile phones are a good example, if you are the only one with a mobile phone then phones are fairly useless, right? We will touch on technological transitions and s-curve adoptions later in the book.

Now, since money is taken out in the form of debt, not only on a personal level but a national level too, it can delay or minimize for a time the effects of inflation, compared to just outright printing money like in Zimbabwe, Venezuela etc, as it can be seen that there is "demand" for the printed US money. As we spoke about already.

More importantly and to the point, since money is taken out in the form of debt, it must be paid back.

So, how the focaccia is it going to be paid back? or is it going to be paid back at all?

Remember, they will have to pay it back to halt inflation spiralling out of control via the lack of need to create new money to fuel the debt repayments and economic growth which has stagnated when you measure it in real economic output sense.

Remember, the consequences of losing purchasing power through no fault of the people will ultimately drive many people to other monetary systems that bring them more/the most amount of value, thus the current power establishment would lose control and power over the monetary system which by extension means the current power establishment would lose power, and that CANNOT be allowed to happen under any circumstance as far as they are concerned.

So, Let's look at the entire macroeconomic picture and not just knit pick 1 or 2 examples. As this will give us the best indication of what is to come.

Let's look at global debt to global GDP ratio:

Global Debt = $400,000,000,000,000 (400 Trillion)   4

-- = ---- as a fraction

Global GDP = $100,000,000,000,000 (100 Trillion)   1

Average interest rate = 3% (govt, corporate and personal debt)

Since the numerator (debt) is 4 times the size of the denominator (GDP), simple maths tells us that just for GDP to keep up with the interest payments of the debt @ 3% p.a. (before you even start looking at paying back the principal), global GDP needs to outgrow the debt at a ratio of 4:1. This means GDP needs to grow at 12% p.a. AND THAT'S JUST TO KEEP UP WITH THE INTEREST PAYMENTS.

Global GDP under any rational circumstance CANNOT and WILL NOT grow at 12% p.a. as it has almost never happened in the history of mankind, let alone for it to happen every year forever, just to keep up with interest payments.

To put the nail in the coffin, the debt being taken out is not used for production (to increase our output and ability to pay back the debt) but rather consumption (decreases our ability to pay debt).

What does this mean?

The writing is on the wall. Everybody knows it.

There is almost no plausible situation where this amount of global debt can be paid back and when you look at who is in charge i.e., the people who caused it. There is no realistic situation where it will be paid back.

The previous example was of global debt, I however think that the main driver of the expansion of the US dollar monetary supply will be US Debt on a mainly Federal level but will also be influenced by State debt and Local Debt conditions.

To talk specifically about the US Federal Debt. US Federal Debt is at a massive number and is also growing at an extremely high rate.

As time goes on, the exact amount of the debt will change but what is quite evident is the fact that the trend is heading in one direction and more importantly we need to understand how because of the simple mathematical forces driving it in that 1 direction.

I will explain here...

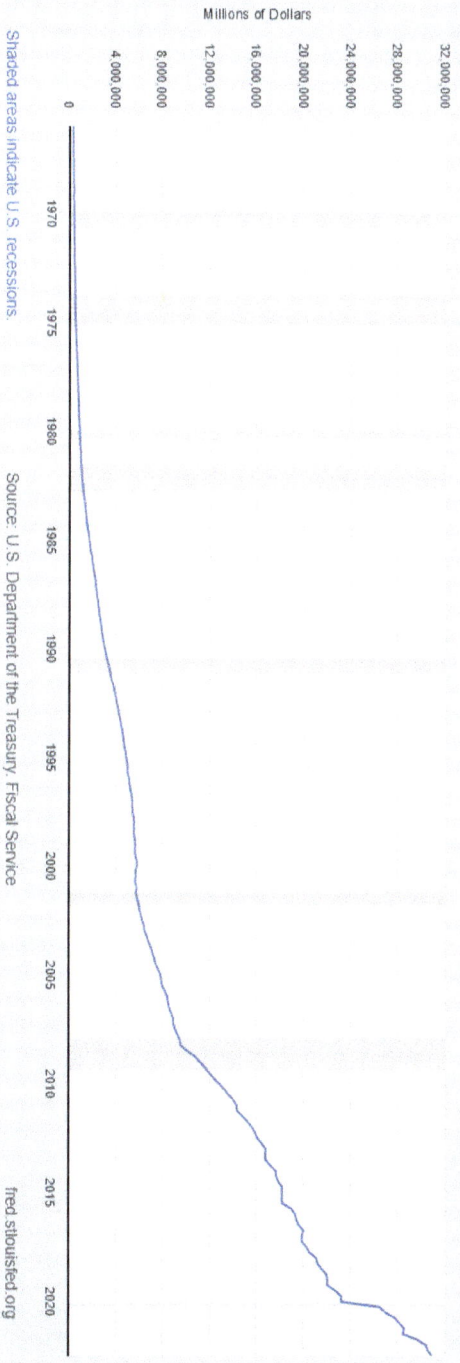

Federal Debt: Total Public Debt

Millions of Dollars

Shaded areas indicate U.S. recessions.

Source: U.S. Department of the Treasury. Fiscal Service

fred.stlouisfed.org

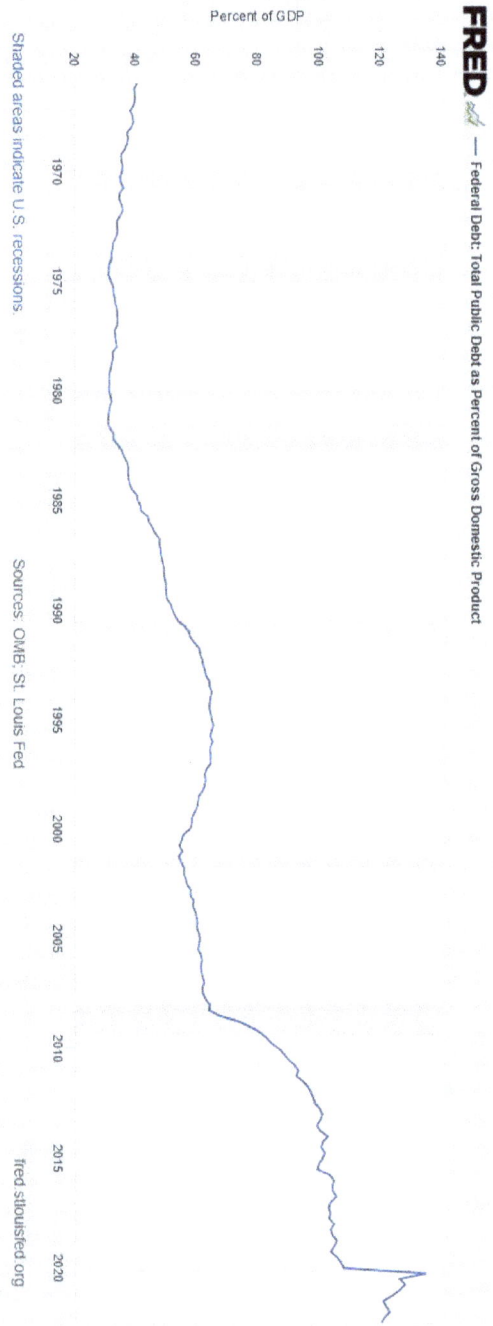

FRED — Federal Debt: Total Public Debt as Percent of Gross Domestic Product

Percent of GDP

Shaded areas indicate U.S. recessions

Sources: OMB; St. Louis Fed

fred.stlouisfed.org

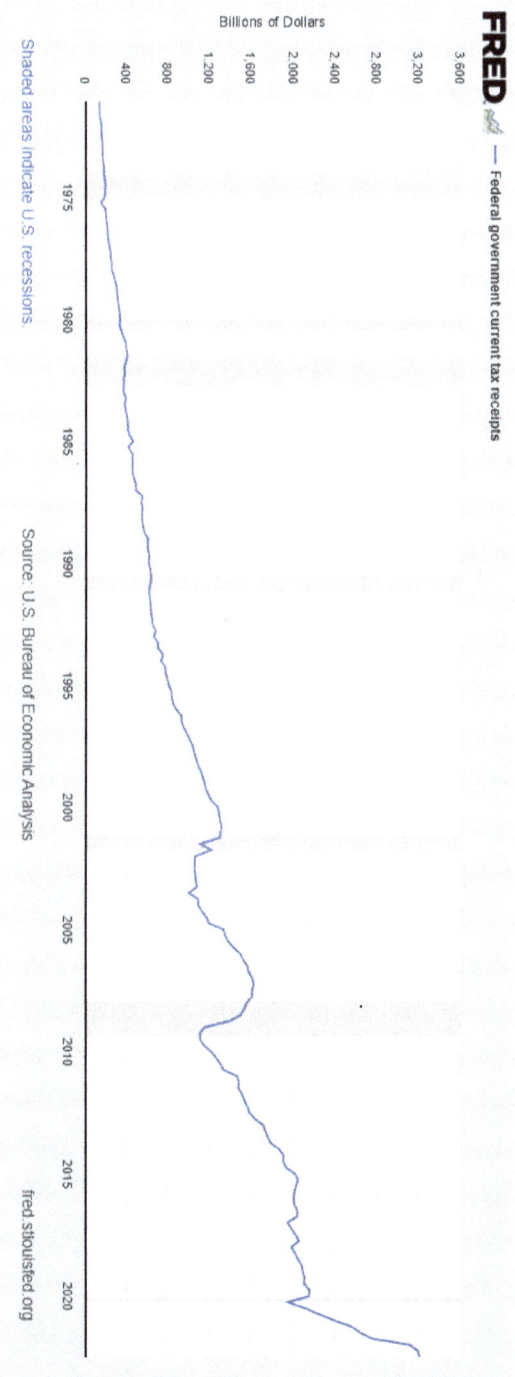

FRED — Federal government current tax receipts

Billions of Dollars

3,600
3,200
2,800
2,400
2,000
1,600
1,200
800
400
0

1975   1980   1985   1990   1995   2000   2005   2010   2015   2020

Shaded areas indicate U.S. recessions.   Source: U.S. Bureau of Economic Analysis   fred.stlouisfed.org

To do some quick maths, we see that national debt has risen from $391 billion dollars in 1971 to $31.5 billion dollars, an 80.56x or 8056% increase. Whereas tax receipts have only grown from $135 billion to $3.2 trillion, a 23.79x or 2379% increase. This means that debt has outgrown tax income by a factor of 3.38.

A scary trend, but will it reverse?

Well, let's look at the factors that go into increasing the ability to pay. Jobs, taxpayers etc.

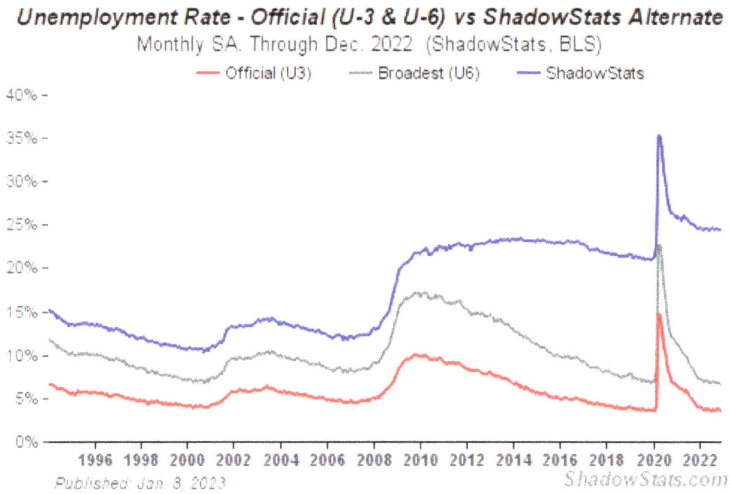

Unemployment Rate - Official (U-3 & U-6) vs ShadowStats Alternate
Monthly SA. Through Dec. 2022 (ShadowStats, BLS)

Published: Jan. 3, 2023 ShadowStats.com

Shadow stats measures the original way that metrics were measured in the 80's. Current statistics for metrics such as unemployment, CPI and pretty much every other government reported metric are manipulated as the government changes the definition/scope of the metric every time the statistic doesn't fit their political narrative.

We see that through the shadow stats, which gives a much fairer representation of unemployment, that the unemployment rate is continually becoming higher and higher and higher on average.

In short, the fewer people working = the fewer tax receipts the government gets = Less money to pay back the debts.

Manufacturing jobs

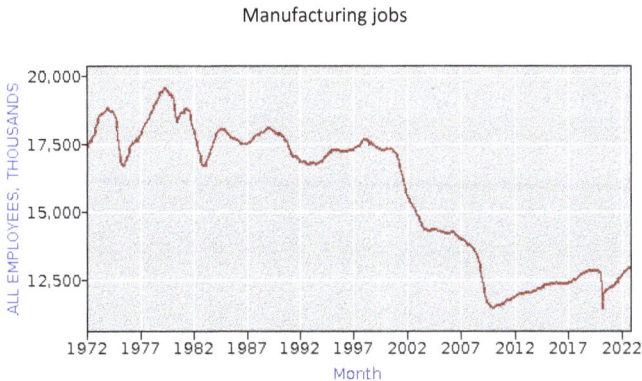

The significance in the reduction is manufacturing jobs is the fact that real economic output of goods is dropping.

This signifies that now more money is fighting over fewer goods and services and the money in the economy is not coming from real economic output.

The economic output has been offshored to other countries who are now gaining the benefits of the real economic output, instead of the USA.

In addition, as mentioned before, fewer jobs = fewer tax receipts = less ability to pay the debt.

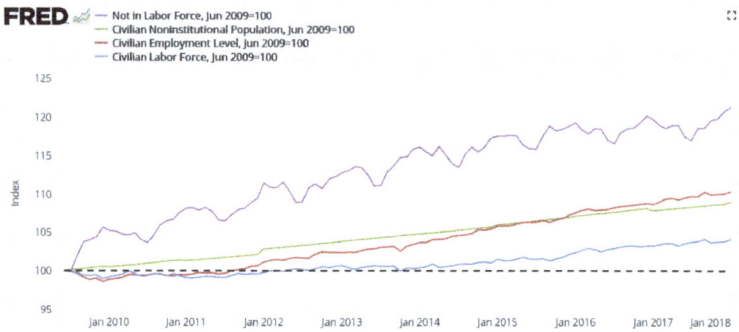

The above chart signifies that people not in the work force grew by 20% between 2010 – 2018.

That's people who have retired or have given up on looking for work.

Where is this chart heading?

The trend is your friend.

Again, the budget items in each annual budget will change in amounts and in % of the budget. The amount of debt will change. The unemployment rate will change. The tax receipts will change. The debt to GDP levels will change. But we see clearly which way the trend is going for all the absolutely vital stats and indicators.

The stats we have seen paint a very clear picture that:

1) Debt levels are rising.
2) Debt is increasing quicker than GDP. I.e., Debt is rising vs GDP

3) Spending is non-productive i.e., not investing in the future.
4) Productivity is decreasing.
5) US workforce is becoming smaller.

So, it paints the picture that debt is rising and the ability to pay it back is shrinking.

You know what the funny thing about all of this is... We haven't even taken into account "unfunded liabilities".

Unfunded liabilities to those unaware, are the debts accrued that haven't been accounted for in the budgets. This can be something like pensions for workers employed by the government which currently stands at over 25 million people. Or medical coverage expected to be needed to be funded by the government.

This number stands at a staggering 170 trillion dollars currently... that's $170,000,000,000,000 dollars.

THE ONLY OPTION TO SUSTAIN THE DEBT IS TO PRINT MORE MONEY!!

The trend of not requiring the printing of massive amounts money is not even close to being on a path of reversing. The only option is to print more money via loans of freshly printed money from the federal reserve in order to pay back existing debts... sounds awfully a lot like *cough* a Ponzi.

Remember too, the only way to prop up this hegemony and physical enforcement of the fiat monetary system is through printing money to pay the enforcers per se. which also remember, becomes exponentially harder as more and more people move to better systems and more and more money is required to pay the enforcers due to the loss of purchasing power.

So how does it play out and when does it happen?

The debts are skyrocketing.

Inflation is skyrocketing.

Even by the feds own admission, CPI (which is a terribly misleading measurement of real inflation as it is a purposely manipulated basket of goods used to measure inflation) is at 8.2% which is well above the fed's "target" of 2%.

Remember inflation is compound. That's 8.2% on the already 643% we have seen since 1971.

Meaning that the inflation is 51.44% of the monetary supply of 1971.

Meaning that for every dollar you had in 1971, you would need $1.51 just to negate the inflation of 2022 alone... Yes, 2022 alone.

Here's a chart to help explain.

53 Year Time Frame:

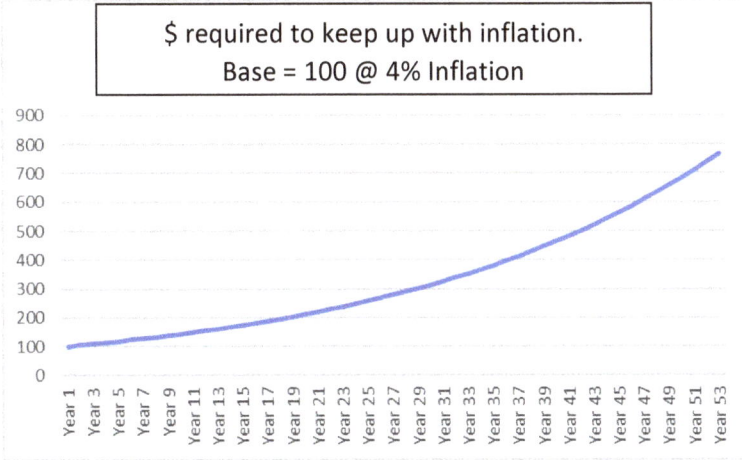

145 Year Time Frame

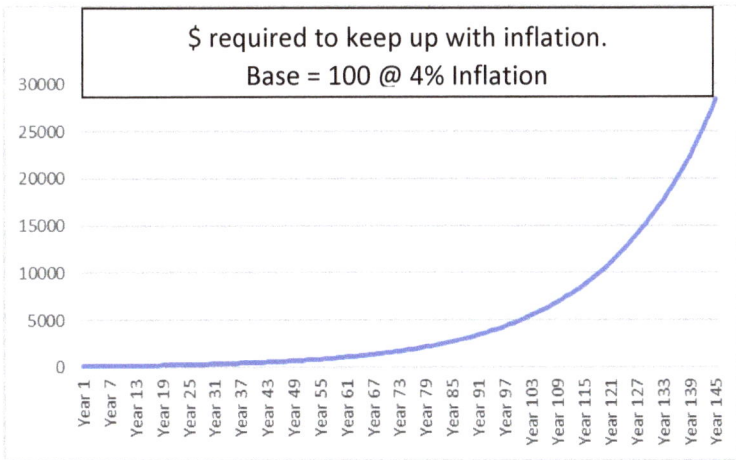

See how it becomes exponential?

This chart is not an exact representation of the exact maths but rather illustrates the mathematical method of what has been happening.

To illustrate just how exponentially worse it becomes on 8% inflation I have added the charts below:

53 Year Time Frame:

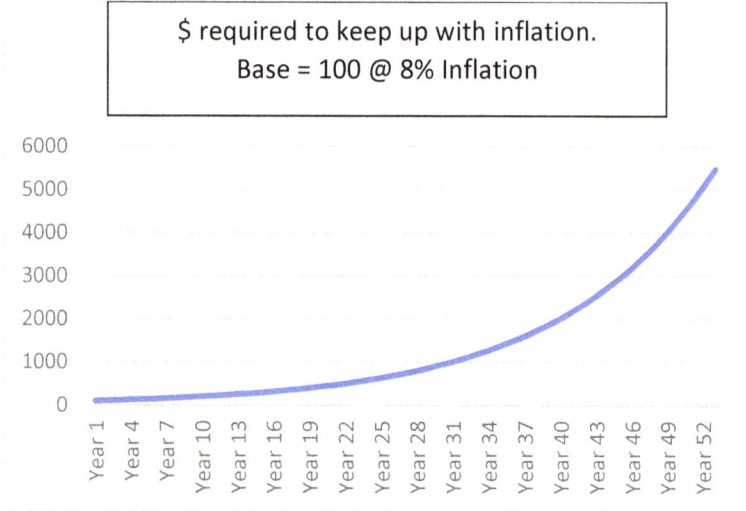

$ required to keep up with inflation.
Base = 100 @ 8% Inflation

145 Year Time Frame:

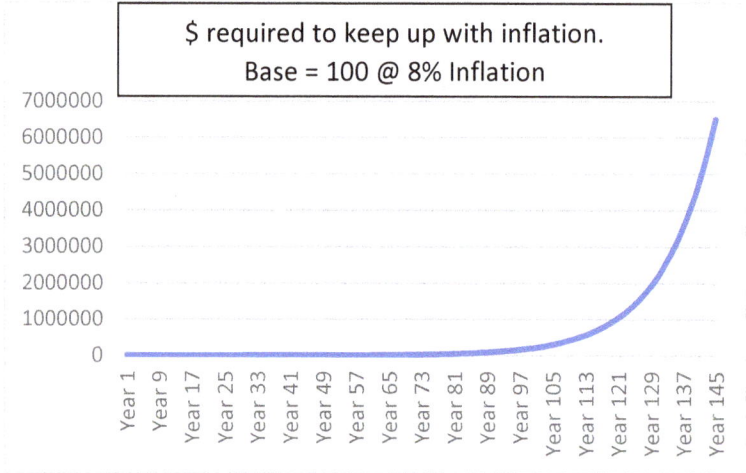

$ required to keep up with inflation.
Base = 100 @ 8% Inflation

YoY Difference in $ Value

$ difference YOY @ 8% Inflation

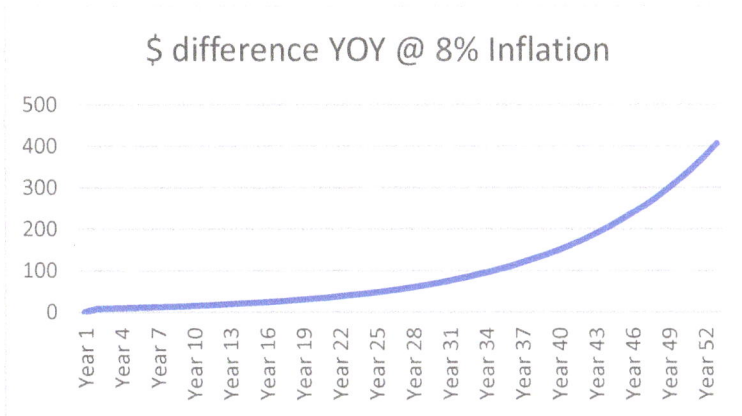

As you can see, you need exponentially more money year over year just to keep up with inflation.

In year 53 of the chart, its more than 50x the inflation in a dollar amount ($405) vs year 1 ($8). Which means the inflation in year 53 alone would have the same impact as 50x inflation in year 1.

A better but still not perfect metric to measure inflation is the shadow stats CPI metric, which is how they measured inflation in the 80's.

According to this method, inflation is approx. 17.5%. and even that is still a manipulated basket of goods.

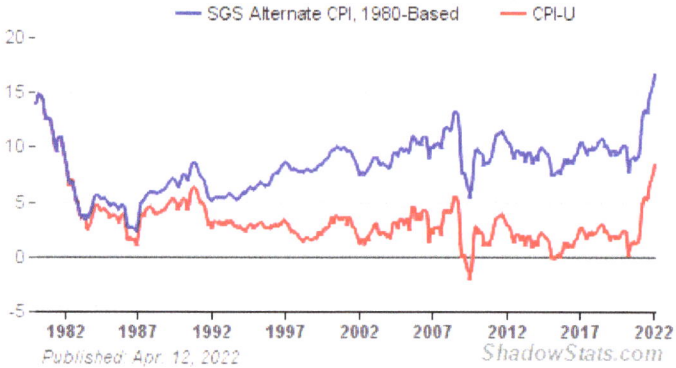

Consumer Inflation - Official vs ShadowStats (1980-Based) Alternate
Year to Year Change. Through Mar. 2022

Real inflation is surely above 20% since the current basket of goods used to measure "inflation" is seriously manipulated.

Can you name one thing (besides your wage) that hasn't gone up or shrunk in size (shrinkflation) at least 20-25% combined in the last year? I can name probably only a handful of goods and services.

Even depreciating assets such as used cars are going up more than 20%.

The government either by malice or ignorance (not sure what's better) are always fabricating "crisis" to "crisis" narratives to blame for the continual poor performance of economic indicators and to justify the printing of money to "stimulate the economy" or as I see it, to fuel their personally motivated political narratives designed to sow strong emotions in one direction or another (love or hate) to then gain votes and move closer to the monetary spigot.

Rather than focusing on what is happening right now, I want this book to be more timeless and relevant as time passes. With that said, examples of narratives that are being used currently to print more money are event such as the War in Ukraine, before that, Covid, before that, 20 years of wars in the middle east. Obviously looking beyond 10 years ago, the 2008 Global Financial Crisis was a very big reason to print money.

We just saw the omnibus bill pass AGAIN which increases borrowing for absolutely ridiculous items such as gender studies in Pakistan (again). It doesn't matter what happens, there will always be a "crisis" which only printing money can prevent. We saw the build back better bill in 2021. All tremendous wastes of money, not increasing the productivity and productive capacity of the nation.

As they say in politics "never waste a good crisis".

So, to answer the question, what is going to happen?

I argue that we are that beginning of hyperinflation which is happening this very second.

The year 2020 was, in my opinion, the "inflection point" that we see in every hyperinflationary event. That is, the point where growth on the Y axis outweighs the growth of the x axis.

Or, put simply, it is when the line goes up faster than it goes sideways.

$ required to keep up with inflation.
Base = 100 @ 4% inflation

Don't believe me?

Look at this.

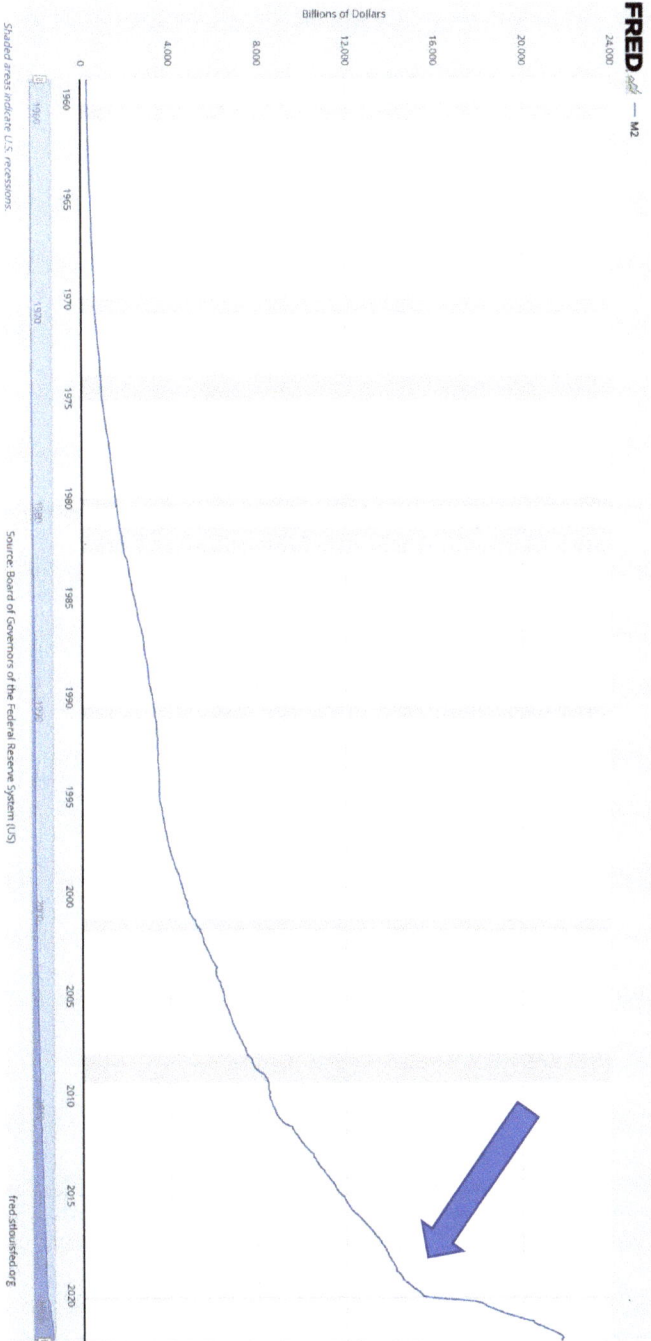

FRED — M2

Billions of Dollars

24,000

20,000

16,000

12,000

8,000

4,000

0

1960   1965   1970   1975   1980   1985   1990   1995   2000   2005   2010   2015   2020

Shaded areas indicate U.S. recessions.

Source: Board of Governors of the Federal Reserve System (US)

fred.stlouisfed.org

A continual rise in the monetary supply over the period since 1971, only to jump in 2020 alone by a factor of 4:1 vs the 1971 supply. As mentioned earlier, they YoY dollar amount increases exponentially as time goes on.

Here is an example of hyperinflation in the Weimar republic (modern day Germany) in the 1920's. The chart is also in logarithmic scale which shows the true craziness of the inflation.

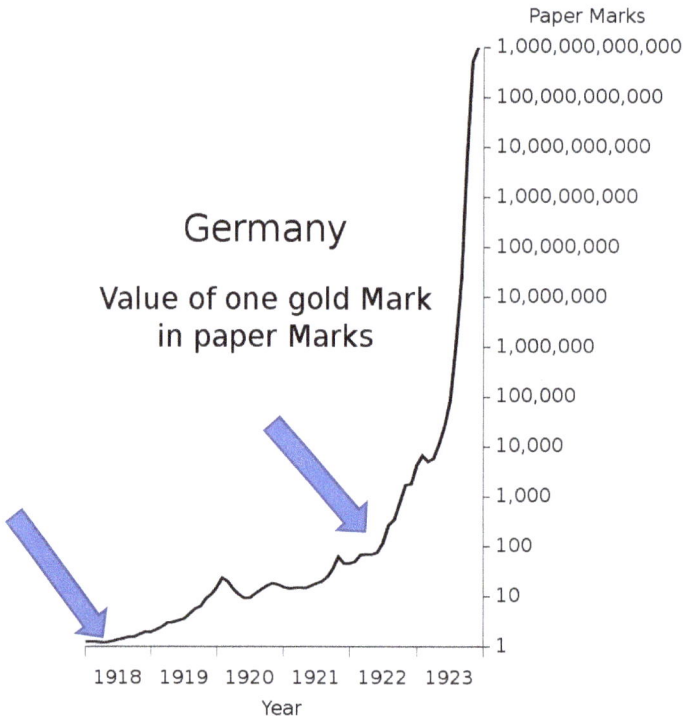

In Weimar republic, the first inflection point came in 1918 when the value of a gold mark went from 1 paper mark 75 paper marks by early 1920.

The second inflection point came at around the 100 paper marks per gold mark in 1922. As you can see, the rest is history.

The years of 1922 and 1923 saw the currency hyperinflate by a factor of 10,000,000,000x (10 billion times the original value) meaning you needed 10 billion marks at the end of 1923 for every 1 mark you had mid-1922. Lol.

As we see not just in this scenario, but all hyperinflationary events, the growth of inflation (monetary supply) is gradually and then suddenly... there becomes a point where it is too late for anyone to attempt to do anything about it. In fact, you can see they tried numerous times with the slight declines in inflation in early 1920, late 1921 and early 1923.

Zimbabwe next.

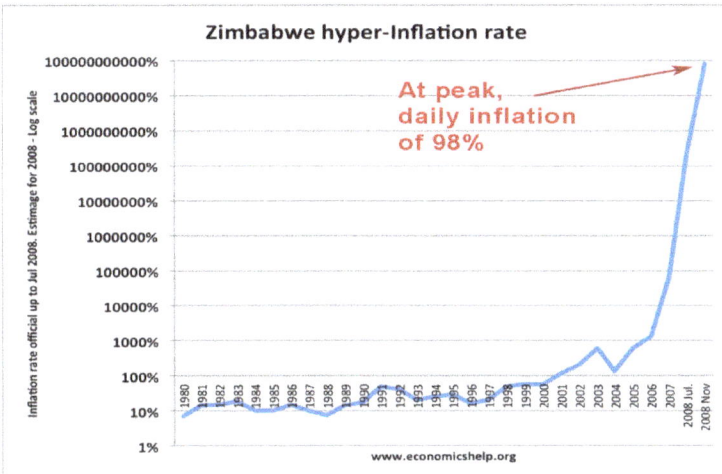

Same cause and same result.

The charts above are also in logarithmic, so you need to take that into account. If it were a normal linear chart, then it would look even more horrific.

Gradually and the suddenly. A process, not an event.

Now, finally let's look at how we know significant inflation at the absolute minimum is coming for the US dollar, if not hyperinflation which is defined as 50% inflation or more per month.

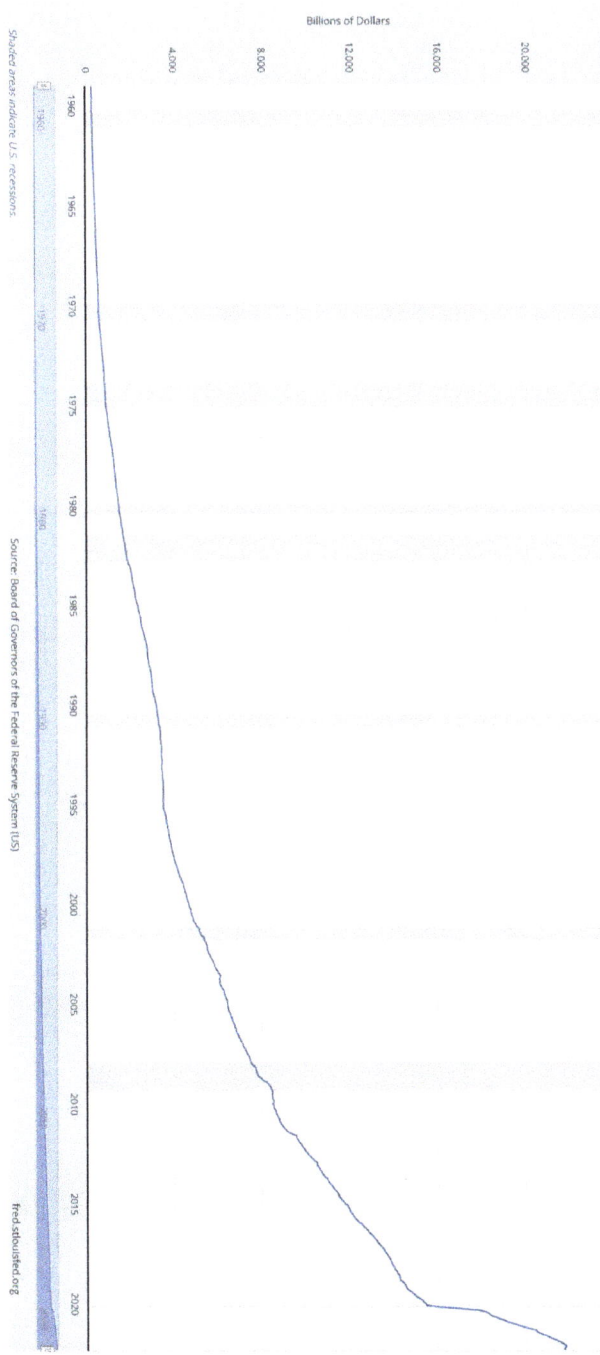

FRED — M2

Billions of Dollars

24,000
20,000
16,000
12,000
8,000
4,000
0

1960 1965 1970 1975 1980 1985 1990 1995 2000 2005 2010 2015 2020

Shaded areas indicate U.S. recessions.

Source: Board of Governors of the Federal Reserve System (US)

fred.stlouisfed.org

This chart shows that the increase in money (inflation) of the US M2 supply is has been gradually and then what, since 2020? Is the start of "suddenly"? This looks like the inflection point, no?

The US dollar has a few tricks up its sleeve that will mean it can survive longer under inflationary pressure than we saw from the currencies of The Weimar Republic and Zimbabwe.

Firstly, the US Dollar is the reserve currency of the world. Meaning it has significantly more artificial demand from other nations as other nations technically need US dollars to settle any foreign transactions and even debts in some cases.

It means that since other countries need US dollars, other countries must obtain US dollars by selling their own currency and hold them (at least for its period of usefulness, which is on a rotating permanent basis) to be able to buy anything from overseas and/or settle debts, whilst the US prints money out of thin air and sells the dollars to other nations in exchange for real goods and services, they are obtaining goods and services for nothing (or at least the cost of paper) and forcing others to hold the currency just as a basic requirement to transact internationally and participate in the global financial system (be able to survive).

This phenomenon is known as "Exporting inflation", as the holders of the devaluing currency are now other nations and not the United States themselves.

Secondly, this on top of the Petro-dollar system where countries are forced to artificially increase the demand of the US dollar by having settle oil transactions in dollars, gives the US dollar and ultimately the US government a sort of hegemony over the rest of the world and certainly an advantage over the currencies that have hyperinflated before it.

This means the US can print dollars and exchange them for oil, essentially forcing other countries to hold their paper whilst obtaining real world goods for it.

As mentioned, debts too are often denominated in US dollars. This can be for a variety of reasons. One reason is because the US Dollar is at least to some extent seen as a "neutral" currency that can't simply be printed by the non US parties in the loan agreement (somewhat trusted since it is the global reserve after all and we do know that normie politicians do like or can at least sell and "argument to authority").

Another reason is if the US loans money to a country, they have enough geopolitical influence to get the other party to accept the terms in US dollars.

The main reason for debt being denominated in US dollars is because the US government is the largest borrower in the world. A trick they use by denominating debt in dollars, is that they can now never default because they have the ability to simply print the dollars out of thin air to pay back its debtors with.

Sure, maybe the US may not ever seriously default but it really becomes a matter of how much those paid back dollars can buy for the debtor. In other words, a country may receive its 1 trillion dollar loan back however what that 1 trillion US dollars will actually buy once its paid back is another question.

These previous examples being Weimar republic and Zimbabwe were only two examples of many currencies that have significantly declined in value throughout history as a result of being backed by absolutely nothing or being debased to a point of decreased value, "fiat" in other words.

In fact, every fiat currency in the history of the world has failed, except the ones that are around today, which are not that old and as expected, are declining at an exponential rate, who would have though? How could this happen again? Lol

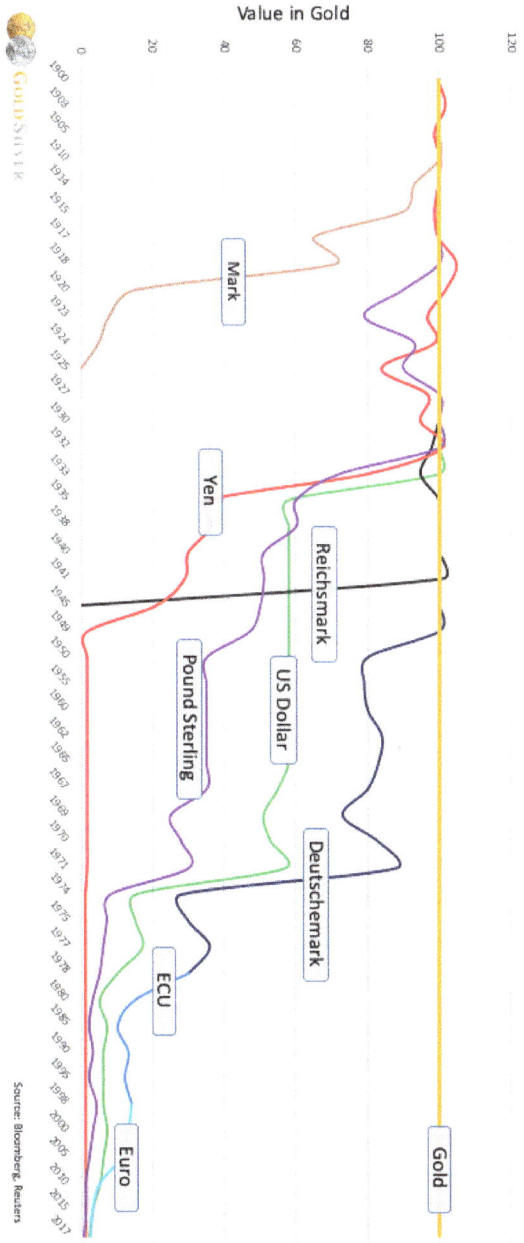

Value in Gold

Gold&Silver

0   20   40   60   80   100   120

1900 1903 1905 1910 1914 1915 1917 1918 1920 1923 1924 1925 1927 1930 1932 1933 1935 1938 1940 1941 1945 1949 1950 1955 1960 1962 1966 1967 1969 1970 1971 1974 1975 1977 1978 1980 1985 1990 1996 1998 2000 2005 2010 2015 2017

Mark

Yen

Reichsmark

Pound Sterling

US Dollar

Deutschemark

ECU

Euro

Gold

Source: Bloomberg, Reuters

To give you an idea of exactly how much fiat currencies are devaluing the chart above has been provided. This really isn't an extensive period of time. In only 120 years, most currencies have lost circa 95-99% of their purchasing power vs gold. Also, at this time I want you to remember the chart we spoke about earlier where you need an exponential amount of money to keep up with inflation.

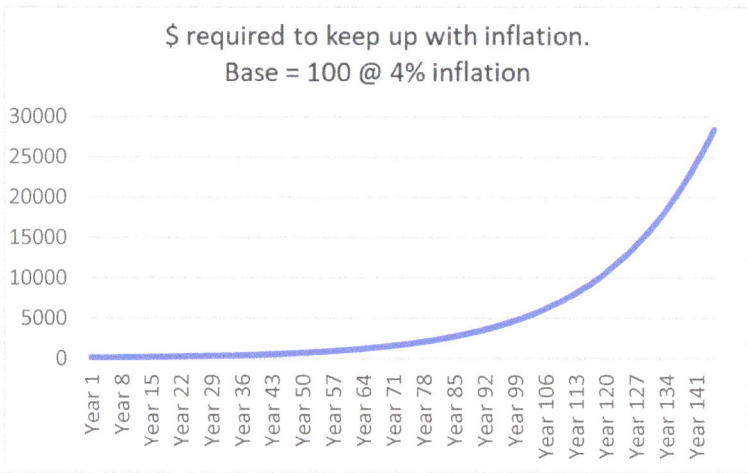

$ required to keep up with inflation.
Base = 100 @ 4% inflation

And a more extended time frame of the US M2 supply; next page

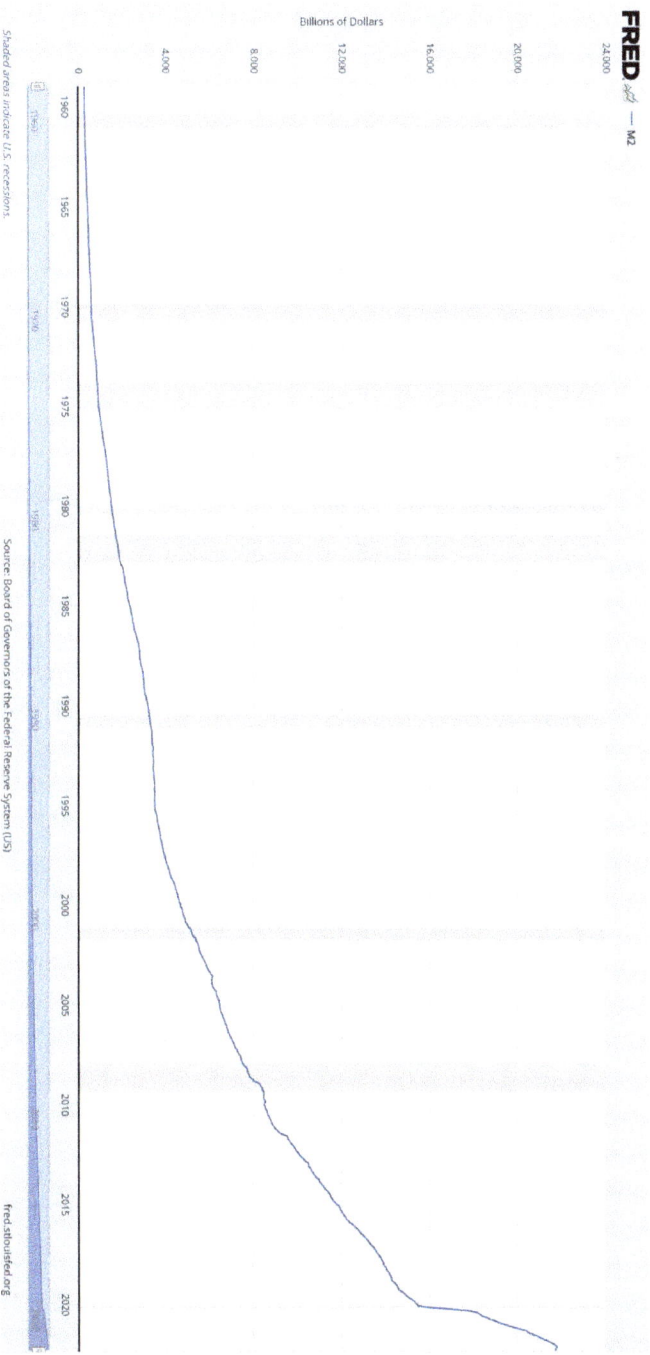

FRED — M2

Billions of Dollars

24,000

20,000

16,000

12,000

8,000

4,000

0

1960 1965 1970 1975 1980 1985 1990 1995 2000 2005 2010 2015 2020

Shaded areas indicate U.S. recessions.

Source: Board of Governors of the Federal Reserve System (US)

fred.stlouisfed.org

Starting to get the picture now of how and why these currencies are becoming exponentially worthless. The above M2 supply only demonstrates since 1959 as no further data was available. Gradually, then suddenly.

Another trick government uses to hide the devaluation of these currencies is how they measure the currencies vs each other in asset trading pairs i.e., USD/EUR, GBP/USD. Rather than measuring the currencies vs real good and services.

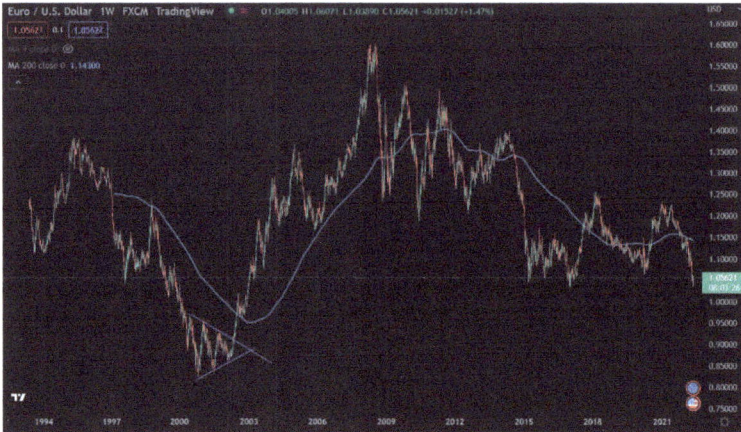

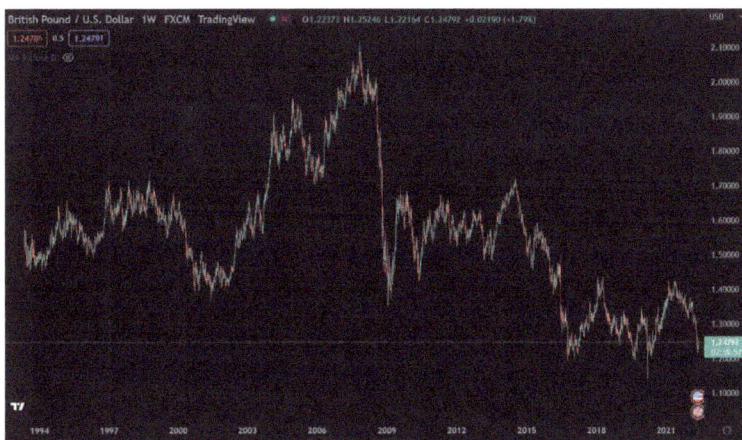

As you see with these fiat vs fiat charts, they just look so much prettier and ultimately, much more stable as they are devaluing at largely the same rate BUT essentially these currencies vs gold are being devalued at an exponential rate.

Why are they devaluing at the same rate? Why do other currencies not outperform the USD when they are just printing money out of nowhere and creating artificial demand? Since prices get their value from supply and demand, why don't traders/holders just call the bluff of the Ponzi and sell for safer, less abundant assets?

The answer is kind of complicated and to sum it up. In short, it is called the **milkshake theory.**

You've made it this far into the chapter, the "milkshake theory" is the last point I will make before moving onto the next chapter.

This is a theory by Brent Johnson, although I don't really think it is a theory, I just see it as basic maths. It refers to a giant liquidity "milkshake" in global markets brought about by the US dollar.

The theory in essence refers to dollars being "sucked up" by foreign markets because as we spoke about earlier, global markets need dollars to settle transactions and to pay debts which ultimately leads to a higher demand for the dollars which in turn leads to the ability of the US being able to print more money through artificial demand created by virtue of being the reserve currency of the world.

But we already spoke about this earlier, didn't we? Yes, we did.

BUT and a big BUT at that... pay attention and don't be scared to read over the next part a few times if you need to.

Because extra demand is created for the US dollar, the other economies around the world are technically performing worse as the demand for and strength of the dollar climbs.

Remember it's just assets vs assets and when everything is measured in dollars, the other currencies technically are worth less dollars as strength for the dollar rises.

So as the dollar rises and since nearly all debts are set in dollars, countries NEED the dollars to pay back their debts and thus scramble to be able to buy more dollars. They do this by printing more of their own currency as the level of their economic output relative to the US dollar dwindles, right at the time that they need it most.

This inevitably leads to a devaluation of the other countries' currencies vs the US dollar and gives more purchasing power to the dollar. The global devaluation spiral begins, this mechanism allows the US to print more dollars to devalue the dollar vs other countries. Creating and entire "milkshake" of global liquidity. This is how the US sucks up global liquidity. In essence, allowing the entire Ponzi to start again and how the US hegemony allows them to get away with enormous amount of stimulus and QE.

But importantly, at the cost of the people who hold dollars (you, me, and everyone we know).

THEY ARE STEALING FROM US, WE ARE THE ONES PAYING FOR THIS.

The entire premise of this chapter was to illustrate to you that fiat currencies, the fiat system and by extension the current global power structure that is propped up because of it, is coming to an end by either means of total devaluation or by the incentive structures that lead people to look for alternatives. It really is just plain mathematics at this point.

You will under every plausible circumstance that I can think of, have to adopt a new money eventually, be it before or after you lose your purchasing power. The choice to adopt a new money is yours. A choice you can make right now as you are reading this. Everyone will buy Monero at the price they deserve.

Exactly when? I don't think anyone can give a categorical answer as all anyone would be trying to do is guess the incredible amount of political, technological, and other variables that may take place.

What we should look for is the signposts along the road.

What are those signposts? Let's look at it in the next chapter.

Chapter 3

Zoom out... see the bigger picture.

Historical & Revolutionary Cycles

Most of society is far too zoomed in on their own lives and as such, view everything on short time scale with a small world view.

Most people are barely sentient and just do what they have been programmed to do, although they may believe they actually are freely choosing to do. However most people are programmed to simply get up go to work, come home to consume the toxic sludge on the TV that controls their perspective and sources of information, eat their toxic fiat food, purchase the products they have been told to purchase and then repeat the next day. A slave class life.

A life of never really questioning anything or going above and beyond to achieve something or live an extraordinary life, as they are too busy being programmed by things like Tik Tok & TV, seeking short term endorphin hits from being distracted constantly. Their behaviours are ultimately being programmed.

What they ultimately miss though is the ability to see the bigger picture and they often refuse to even admit it exists, as they are so far zoomed in on their life and what is in front of them. Most people literally cannot even see what has been or what will be coming. They only see what is in front of them.

In this chapter, I am going to cover the various short and long timeframe cycles. Cycles that range from economic and social cycles to complete revolutions.

Right now, and in the coming years, we are really at a historically important moment. Although, I know it doesn't necessarily seem like it at the moment. However, it never really does seem important though, until we look back and realise the full extent of what was going on.

We have many different cycles converging at this 1 point in history. It is truly set to be a very unique time in history. What a time to be alive. What a time to be gaining knowledge to position yourself at the front of the greatest transformation of wealth in the history of the world.

We have **short and long term debt cycles** converging to create a large decline in economic productivity and output. As illustrated below.

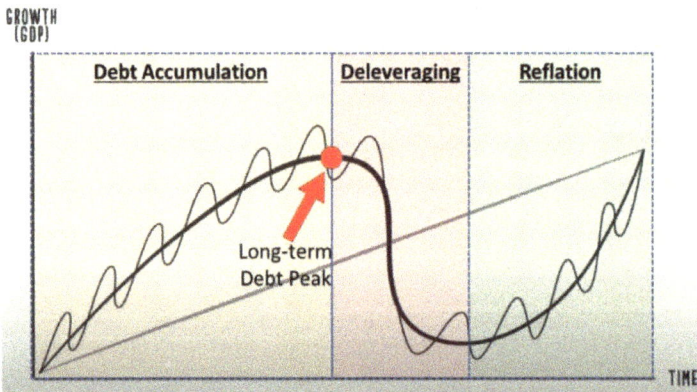

We have The **Generational cycles** that create good and bad times due to the various upbringings, attitudes and experiences of 4 different generations. Called the **Fourth Turning**. Summed up briefly in the illustration below.

HARD TIMES
CREATE STRONG MEN

WEAK MEN
CREATE HARD TIMES

∞

STRONG MEN
CREATE GOOD TIMES

GOOD TIMES
CREATE WEAK MEN

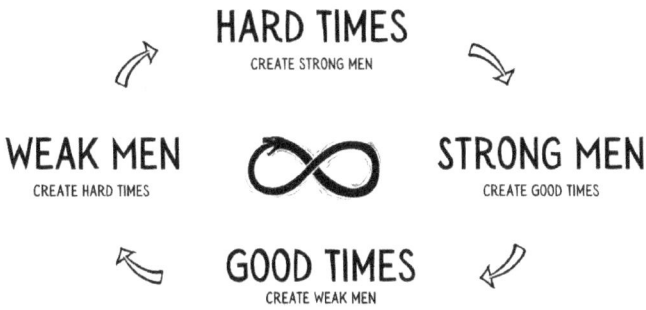

And we have the 3 Harbingers of Revolution

1. 50 Year Technological Revolution cycle
2. 80 Year Populist uprising Cycle
3. 250 Year Empire Revolutionary Cycle

The Three Harbingers of Revolution

All Cycles Converge in 2017

250-Year Revolutionary Cycle
84-Year Populist Movement Cycle
28-Year Financial Crisis Cycle

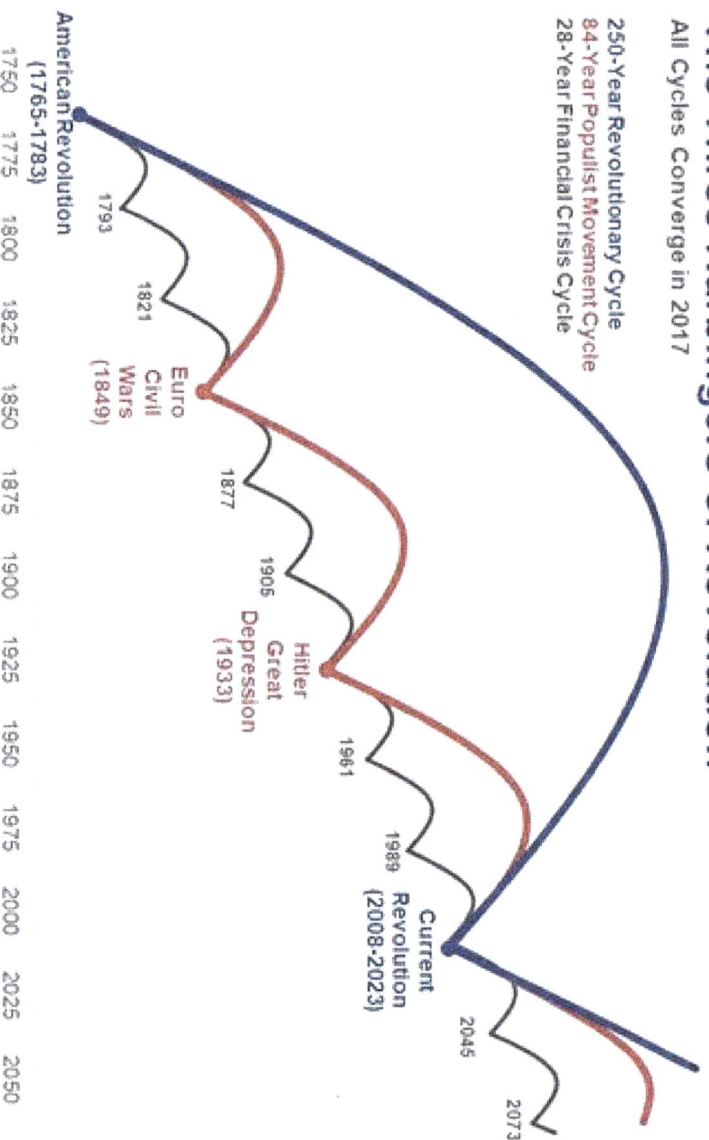

American Revolution
(1765-1783)

1750 1775 1800 1825 1850 1875 1900 1925 1950 1975 2000 2025 2050

1793

1821

Euro
Civil
Wars
(1849)

1877

1905

Great
Depression
(1933)

Hitler

1961

1989

Current
Revolution
(2008-2023)

2045

2073

All very interesting cycles that are bound to shape the world as we see it, in the coming years. We will cover these cycles in depth and explain how they will shape the world and contextualize how all these cycles will lead to Monero being the solution for a much more stable, free, prosperous, and peaceful world.

So, let's dive right in, starting with **short and long term debt cycles**.

It's no secret that the ultimate bible to understanding these cycles is Ray Dalio's: How the Economic Machine Works.

I will not go into as much detail as is available via that piece of work in this book, as it would cover 200 pages alone. I will however cover the major concepts and relay this back to how it affects civilisation in the coming years.

The short and long term debt cycles refer to how the amount of debt in an economy affects productivity and growth.

About two-thirds of a country's growth rates will be due to productivity and about one-third will be due to debt. In essence, giving you a 1.5x multiplier due to debt. I.e., meaning that the economic output increases by 50% more than normal.

The problem however is that debt needs to be paid back. As Dalio states, current debt is future productivity. Debt can only be paid back with future productivity. So, you are sacrificing future productivity in favour of current productivity or consumption, based on the debt taken out.

In other words, when you borrow money today, you are temporarily increasing your buying power, ultimately trading off your future buying power due to repayments that will need to be made, which means you will have less money in the future.

Buying something you cannot afford via credit means that you are spending more than you make. You are borrowing not only from the lender of credit but also from your future productivity i.e., your future self. When it becomes systemic like it is today, due to the availability of credit from the ability to create money out of thin air for lending, Increases and decreases in credit availability serve as a main driver of economic growth/activity as well as contractions/recessions, respectively.

The short term cycles occur on a roughly 8-10 year basis, characterised by the short term bubbles and declines in localised and individual markets. Meanwhile, long term debt cycles occur on a 75-100 year basis, characterised by the gradual increases in economic factors such as standard of living, due to credit expansion. Then the monumental economic declines caused by the reallocation of money. During all of this, real economic growth/ productivity growth remains more or less constant.

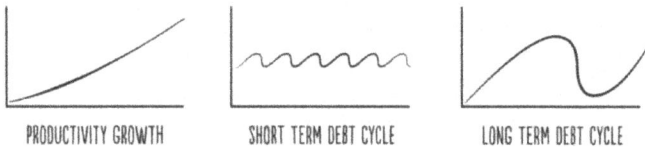

PRODUCTIVITY GROWTH   SHORT TERM DEBT CYCLE   LONG TERM DEBT CYCLE

As humans, we are naturally able to see short term cycles more than we are able to see long term cycles (If indeed we see them at all). The way the human brain works is that it focuses on what happened recently, I suppose we could write a book as to why. Consequently though, it means that for the most part, we are incapable of seeing the huge bubble that is the economy.

The long-term debt cycle is made up of many short-term debt cycles (of which, most people just remember the last one i.e., the last decade or so) . Long term debt crises occur when the cost of servicing the debt rises ever rapidly to a point where it become unsustainable to support the debt, the naturally allowing for and needing a deleveraging event.

What are we seeing at the moment? Well, it's pretty obvious given the chart on the next page.

Millions of Dollars

FRED — Federal Debt Total Public Debt

Shaded areas indicate U.S. recessions

Source: U.S. Department of the Treasury, Fiscal Service

fred.stlouisfed.org

As we have already thoroughly explored, US federal debt is spiralling out of control; it is becoming exponential. National Debt to GDP is at 137% (sept 2022) meaning for every dollar of productivity there is 1.37 Dollars of debt (Just for Federal Government debt)

Again, the current amount of unfunded liabilities is approximately $ 171,000,000,000,000 dollars (Sept 2022) leaving it at 712% of current GDP.

With the debt becoming exponential, it is only a matter of time before a deleveraging event takes place. IT HAS TO. It's just maths. This means that ultimately, the door for another reserve asset to come along an take its place is wide open. What is going to exist after the dollar?

Make no mistake, Lending and borrowing are by no means a bad thing, nor are they inherently bad for the economy. In fact, when done right, lending and borrowing allow for the most efficient allocation of capital in the economy and society.

It is however, poison to create money out of thin air to facilitate the creation of credit. Or the opposite, create credit out of thin air to facilitate the creation of money.

When we look at the problems created by credit creation, we should look to avoid them in the future. In case it's not clear I will address what the problems are.

- The ability to create and maintain a monetary system that steals from everyone and redistributes arbitrarily based on the decision of a few powerful elites.
- The ability to create an elite ruling class that dictates the lives of the rest of the entire world based on the creation of money and how that money is siphoned to that ruling class. At the end of the day, money is power.

- The ability to create naturally unsustainable laws, rules, policies and doctrines that do not benefit anyone except the creators. It is through the ability to create and control the monetary system that these laws are now "sustainable" or able to be kept in place for extended periods of time. The alternative to this is that governments have to convince the population that the laws are worth spending money on, thus need to have the financial backing of the people to sustain it via taxes.

With the door opening, we should look to adopt a new currency that allows for the maximisation of freedom and is as resistant as possible to tyranny or control.

The next chapter will go into detail about the exact reasons that Monero is the best tool we have as a species to fight tyranny and permanently instil lasting freedom & prosperity for all of mankind through the creation of an equal and fair playing field from which to build and produce.

In short however, the decentralization of Monero allows it to be controlled by no one and rather controlled by everyone, creating a system where everyone gets an equal say in the monetary system of their choice. This means that many of the tricks used in the fiat system such as credit creation out of thin air, which leads to the short and long term bubbles, resulting in the devastation of who almost always ends up being the working class, is not possible.

The privacy of the transactions and all data associated with that i.e., user data, balances and linking KYC data. Very briefly, means it is heavily resistant to state level attacks against the protocol and its users, Unlike Bitcoin and by extension every other "crypto" coin on the market. That is one of my main contentions against the use of Bitcoin as freedom money, is its lack of real resilience against coordinated global attacks from state actors who will go to any length to maintain the current power structure. A state actor can still implement dystopian policies such as a social credit system and a broader digital panopticon through the 100% transparency of the blockchain, which is there for the entire world to see.

Thus, I digress. We will cover it more in the next chapter.

The next cycle to take into account is the fourth turning generational theory.

The fourth turning essentially refers to the 4 stages of a society and its prosperity or therefore lack of it according to the generation since the last reformation.

generally speaking , it goes as follows:

1) Hard times create strong men.
2) Strong men create good times.
3) Good times create weak men.
4) Weak men create hard times.

Thus, the cycle repeats.

It is my contention and the contention of many others that we are in the final stage of the fourth turning at the moment.

1940 - 1960 – Coming out of WW2, an emphasis was put on peace and productivity to grow the nations out of the ashes and destruction of WWII. Hard times created strong people. These years were brought about by incredibly hard times, being the great depression and WW2. Post WW2, there was an incredible amount of genuine economic productivity (not the financialization of the economy that we see today) and innovation of new technologies.

1960 - 1980 – Economic Boom and prosperity, of which the likes had not been seen before. These few decades brought an incredible amount of technology to the masses that had never been thought possible just a century earlier. TV's, Automobiles, Air transport.

Strong people created these good times. There was however, in these times, the start of the wasting of money through pointless wars (Korea & Vietnam) based on political doctrines sponsored by politicians who sought to gain influence from the ability to rile up a population based on what is almost exclusively lies and mistruths.

This era also saw the decoupling of the dollar from the gold standard, which as time will prove (even up until this point) has been the creation and also the death kiss for the fiat monetary system.

1980-2000 – Decoupling from the gold standard started to take its toll and society has started to lose its respect for productivity as a mechanism to create wealth and rather opted for simply printing money.

The financialization of the economy has begun at this point, relying of GDP growth from the creation of money which in turn pumps up the prices of assets, giving the illusion of growth. Whereas in fact, in a purchasing power sense, no productivity or even prices of assets have gone up at all. Good times from the previous decades had created weak people.

2000-2020 – while many technological advances happened, society as a whole started to become more divided. Many freedoms have been lost in favour of "safety". Many economic and social projects have been made not possible due to the incredible amount of burdensome regulations and manmade difficulties.

Many problems have been created by weak people who are in fact under the delusion that they are being "strong". Importantly too, a lot of the economic activity during this period has come from the financialization of the economy rather than genuine productive economic output.

This theory does not in any way contribute to the thesis that ONLY Monero can be the solution but rather shows us that through the hard times that are being created, solutions will be required to help us build towards prosperity once again.

The distortion of money has led to many of the distortions that we see in society today. One of the key innovations to get us out of the distorted world that we currently see will be fixing the money. The saying within the hard money communities is "Fix The Money, Fix The World".

The censorship resistance and decentralisation of Monero will mean that as a society we can all build from an equal playing field and we can seek equally for opportunities without many of the hinderances created and enforced solely by the ability to create money out of thin air. We will get into how this is possible in the next chapter, but for now, next Cycle.

The following cycle "The 3 harbingers of revolution" has been largely inspired by the works of Mark Moss and Ray Dalio.

Human action in general is very predictable and repetitive, thus by looking at history and the revolutions & development that have happened in the past, we can take that information and map it out to make future forecasts about what we think is going to happen with very strong accuracy. History doesn't repeat, it rhymes.

Historically speaking, we have seen big changes and developments occur on a largely predictable and constant basis. These changes usually occur on 50 Year, 80 Year and 250 Year cycles. All 3 of which are 3 different cycles:

- 50 Year Technological Revolution
- 80 Year Political/societal Revolution
- 250 Year empire Revolution

The 50, 80 and 250 Year cycle thesis is probably the most important factor in regard to the massive change we will see in the coming years/decades.

-

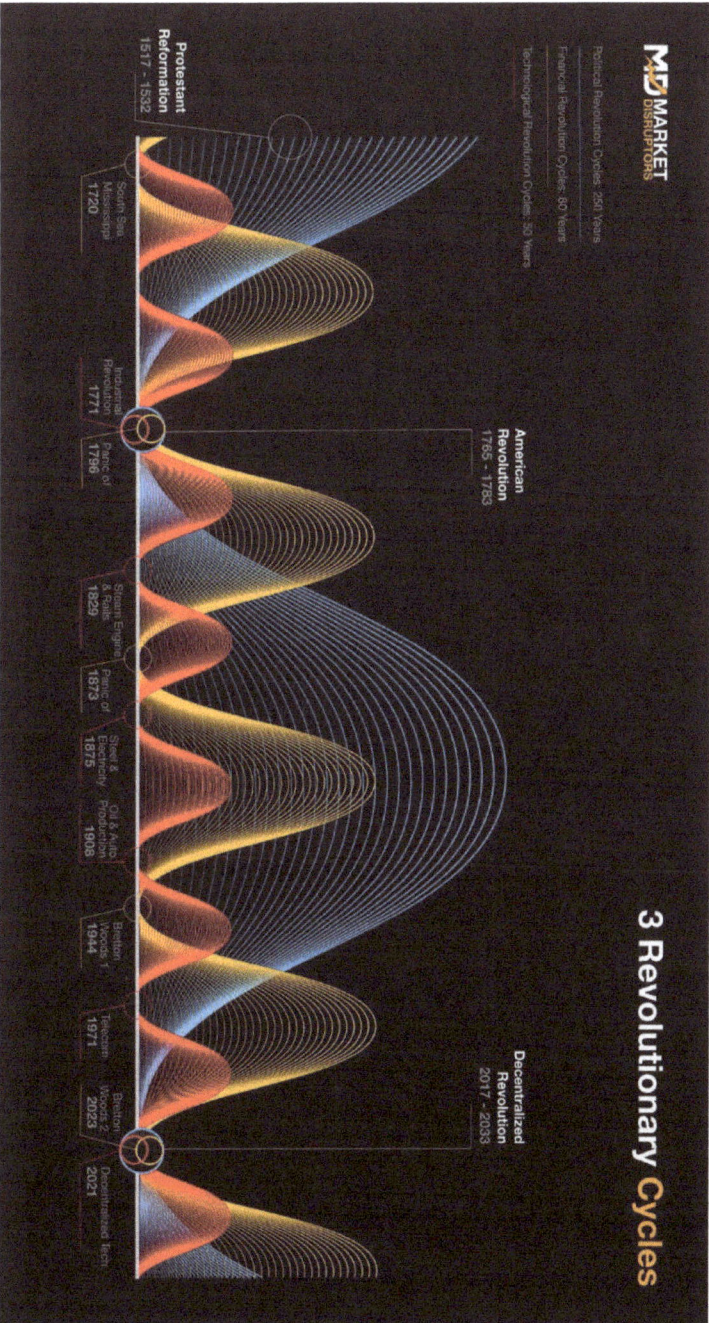

3 Revolutionary Cycles

50 Year Technological Revolutions

Technological developments have shaped the course of humanity as we know it over and over again throughout history. It is perhaps what separates us from every other life form on earth.

There is a distinct difference between technological advancements and technological revolutions. The iPhone is an example of a technological advancement, sure it's cool and it helps you in new ways, but it doesn't do the following 2 things.

> 1) It doesn't change the course of history and

> 2) It doesn't drive financial markets.

Those are the 2 key features of a technological revolution.

One thing that has remained constant, or at least semi constant is the cycles at which "revolutionary" technological advancements happen. Every 50 years (generally speaking) we have technological revolutions.

2010's Decentralized technology ????

1960's Computing & Microprocessors

1910's Oil, Petrol engines & Mass Production

1860's Electricity, Steel & Heavy engineering

1820's Steam & Railways

1770's Industrial Revolution, Wrought Iron & Machinery

Beyond the technological cycles, there are financial cycles which generally run parallel in which capital inflows into these innovations happens, which allows for the utilization of capital to maximise the potential benefits reaped from the technology. As mentioned without this, it cannot be considered a revolution.

These stages are:

1) Eruption phase: The stage generally involves large amounts of funding into new technologies. New use cases appear . New industries are established on the use cases in which have been deemed economically viable, and the construction of new infrastructure begins.

2) Frenzy phase: Increased speculation and financialization based on greed leads to the decoupling between financial valuations and productive output of the new technology. Assets are inflated to a bubble-like market structure.

3) Synergy phase: A need for political regulation of the financial sector is acknowledged based on the magnification of negative effects of over financialization and over speculation. Asset bubbles may burst during this period. The link between financial valuations and production valuations moves closer to the equilibrium/fair value.

4) Maturity phase: The market for the new technology begins to become saturated. Due to increased technological knowledge and market participation. Society at large adopted the new technologies. Opportunities for investment have become standard low yield traditional industries. Financial capital is moving into new innovations and new regions where it may lay the foundation of the next great surge.

Judging by the historical trends, we were due for a technological innovation in the 2010's. As you can see the technologies often build on top of one another and compliment the previous technology, these are not technological revolutions though. Technological revolutions completely overhaul and shake up existing societal infrastructure all together.

It is my contention that the innovation that changed the world going into the future from here is decentralized technology and more specifically, decentralized money. Decentralized money takes the immense power of the monetary spigot out of the hands of a small group of elites for the first time in the history of the world.

This is a very unique time in history because for the first time ever, the individual is being completely powered to engage in any commercial or personal interests he or she deems fit to a productive society.

Whilst engaging in it in a private capacity, there is not a person who can do a damn thing about it. We could obviously write an entire book on the power of decentralized technology as a whole, however we won't.

80 Year Cultural and Social Revolutions

The 80 year revolution cycles are arguably some of the most world changing developments in a generational/lifetime sense.

Let's look at some of the biggest events in world history that have occurred on these cycles.

2020's Rise up against globalism???

1940's: Hitler & WW2

1860's: American Civil War

1780's American Revolution & French Revolution

1700's War of Spanish succession

These political/cultural revolutions are brought about generally by a slow build-up of oppression in society that favours few whilst disadvantaging and severely limiting the vast majority of people.

The oppression itself, often comes in many different forms but the important thing to remember is the decline in freedoms and standards of living that leave populations with few options but to stand up against their oppressors who are ultimately benefiting far too much from the oppression of others to change the system itself.

All the events listed above for the previous 250-300 years are caused exactly by this. Oppression beyond acceptable means.

For example, Why I have included WW2 and not WW1 is because Hitler and by extension WW2 were caused by the oppression of Germany and the German people post WW1. Whereas WW1 was caused by empires simply becoming too large to a point where it was inevitable that they would "slug it out". It was not any populace who caused WW1 but rather the empires and egos themselves.

250 year political/empire Revolutionary cycle

Looking at the past 500 years there have been 2 major events that have definitely shaped the direction of the world more than others. In short, the first event was the protestant reformation/the separation of church and state in the early 1500's, which was heavily influenced by the invention and impact of the Gutenberg printing press and subsequently the publication of the Ninety-five Theses by Martin Luther in 1517, beyond this specific example,a greater "enlightenment" period also followed the invention of the Gutenberg printing press.

The second event approximately 250 years later was the American war of independence and the establishment of the United States of America, which established the first constitutional republic. The foundation of the USA very much shapes the world we see today, as has probably been made quite obvious thus far when talking about the US centric world that we live in.

2020??? Decentralized revolution?

1770's – American Revolution & French Revolution

1520's – Protestant Reformation & The separation of church and state

The events on a large time frame, moved the world towards freedom and decentralization of power more than any other events in my view.

In all empires, we see many different variables and outcomes however they almost always follow the same pattern of events in roughly 30 year periods. The stages are as follows:

1) Outburst – Following the establishment of a new to be empire, the people are largely happy to be free and have achieved their goals. Their newly found freedoms have enabled them to live their life as they see fit and this expands to many areas of society, not just an individual happiness. New industries and ways of life start emerging and thriving under the newly found liberties. Often, the most common job/occupation is being a pioneer.

2) Conquest – Following the original establishment, every to be empire goes through a period of conquest and expansion. Often the most common job at the time is a soldier or officer in the armed forces. Subsequently, the empire begins to be ruled by generals and military men.

3) Commerce – Following expansion, new economic opportunities and resources become available. This naturally

sees a period of increased wealth and prosperity due to the expansion of economic opportunities available. Often, the most common job is a merchant or trader.

4) Affluence – Businessmen and merchants who normally value material success and dislike taking unnecessary risks—take over at the highest levels of society. Their societies downplay the values of the soldier and the values which gave increased prosperity and opportunity.

5) Intellect – "intellectuals" and think tanks begin to take over due to the loss of the need to be attached to productive process' and experience hard times. They have become completely detached from the values of what built the empire. These intellectuals often theorise utopian societies and what it would be like to live in the perfect world. Academia is a common profession.

6) Decadence – After over a century of facing few challenges and all living decades becoming detached from the principles of what made the empire great, the empire itself begins to splurge on completely unnecessary goods and services due to having the wealth accumulated by previous generations. This way of life is seen as totally normal and the decisions to spend excessively on non-productive assets are seen as logical evolutions.

7) Decline - Increasing numbers of people lack the virtues and zeal necessary to work and contribute. The suffering and the sacrifices that built the culture are now a distant memory. As discipline and work increasingly seem "too hard," dependence grows. The collective culture now tips in the direction of dependence. Suffering of any sort seems intolerable. But virtue is not seen as the solution. Having lived on the sacrifices of others for years, the civilization now insists that "others" must solve their woes. This ushers in growing demands for governmental, collective solutions. This in turns deepens dependence, as solutions move from personal virtue and local, family-based sacrifices to centralized ones.

8) Collapse - The corrosive effects of material success encourage the upper class and the common people to discard the self-confident, self-disciplined values that helped to create the empire. Then the empire eventually collapses. Perhaps an outside power, such as the so-called barbarians in Rome's case, wipes it out. Or maybe an energetic internal force, such as the pro-capitalist reformers in the Soviet Union, finishes the job instead. Common jobs during this period are actors and creators of entertainment. In essence, the population is completely detached from almost all rational thought processes.

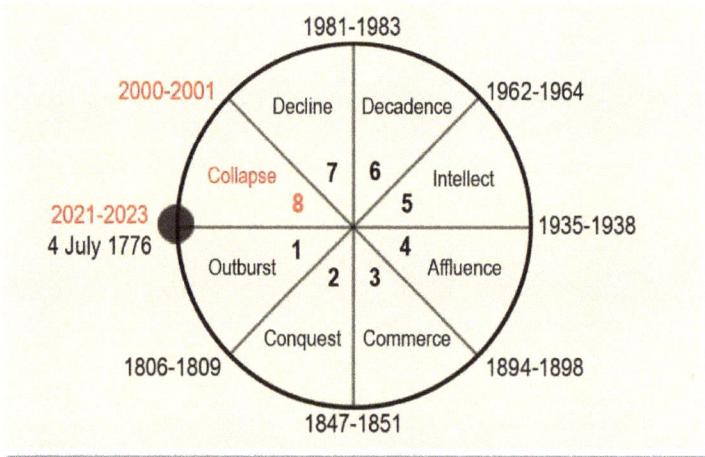

You will have noticed by the dates given that all 3 cycles are converging at this point in history, circa 2010 - 2030. The technological revolution being blockchain, the financial revolution being decentralized money away from fake fiat money and the empire revolution cycle moving away from the dominant world power being the USA who is fuelled by the fake fiat money.

These 3 cycles converging at the same time mean that there is going to be massive change in many aspects of the world as we know to today, breaking them down logically we can see that:

1) **The technological cycle** from computers and microprocessors has become totally mainstream, we have already seen the eruption, frenzy, synergy and now the maturity phase of this technology. The largest companies in the world are technology companies such as Google, Microsoft, Apple and Amazon as a few examples. The area from which they can continue to grow and expand is minimal in a capital appreciation sense. Will they still be around? Yes, of course in my view. They can continue to improve upon products and capitalize on human trends, however the point is that the real era of disruptive innovation is over in this department. Pretty much everything we have uses computers or microprocessors of some description. How much can this continue to grow? And what is the next innovation?

2) **The 80 year populist uprising** is taking place in the form in the ever growing resistance to the encroachment on individual freedoms. More and more segments of society are becoming resistant to the ever growing and over burdensome powers of the globalist agenda and US policy regarding many areas of domestic and international policy. The post WW2 era left the US as the world power and from which many over burdensome policies have been established. The population at large is becoming more aware and increasingly intolerant of the overburdensome regulations that unnecessarily and illogically dictate many aspects of life. These conditions historically speaking, have been very big motivators for populist uprisings/revolutions.

3) **The 250 year empire cycle** is coming to an end... The current global powerhouse being the United States is a dwindling empire, which has many of the top signals historically associated with the downfall of an empire. Complacency & decadence via an ever increasing amount of debt that relies solely on the ability to print money out of thin air to sustain it, economic decline (subtracting the financialization of the economy), the use of fiat currency, division and fracturing of

groups and populations within the broader society, the fact that the leaders are slowly but surely becoming more incompetent, normalisation of corruption within politics, rigging of the democratic process (duopoly), the growing disrepair of the infrastructure, the subversion of society towards useless skills and priorities whilst moving away from useful skills and priorities as STEM fields which have historically developed quality of life and prosperity on a societal if not global level.

The decentralization of money is quite literally a world first, and possibly the greatest evolutionary tool in the history of mankind as it irrevocably provides tools towards human freedom and individual liberty, meaning that the time of tyrants is over. The only way from now on is to provide value in a free market. Meaning that if you don't provide value (I.e., be a tyrant) then you will have no mean by which to collect money and fuel your tyrannical regime.

The decentralization of money provides a revolution for all 3 of these cycles as follows:

1) **Technological revolution**: The invention of decentralized technology is the next step in regard to providing a technology that radically changes the course of what is possible within a global society and also provides a previously unseen and new benefit to the users of the technology. The technology provides significantly more advantages to those who use it vs those who don't.

2) For a **populist revolution:** In the ever increasing world that relies on technology. Decentralized technology counters far beyond any technology that has been implemented to oppress the population. Decentralized technology is a tool that outpowers the current tools used by the establishment and global power structure that are used to implement their authority over the population in general. From nearly all aspects of life. Probably most importantly, it takes the power of money out of the hands of the global power structure and puts it back into the hands of the people. But this time, forever

3) **Empire revolution:**
As we saw from the previous big cycle revolutions, the technologies and events that took place trended the world towards the freedom and prosperity for all. Which if prosperity, happiness and being able to provide for yourself and your family is not what life is about, then what is? Decentralized technology provides a mathematically certain platform from which the world and people can conduct themselves as they see fit. Not beholden to any inevitable human greed/control mechanism which has traditionally been used to control the masses via money for the benefit of a few. The new global empire consists not of any traditional power structure which uses centralized authorities to govern but rather a power structure which allows everyone to govern equally. From this, the current global empire in the US and any further would be global power structure would lose many of its weapons that have traditionally been used to implement the power structure i.e., Money & the control of human interaction.

Despite having corrections away from freedom within these time frames, it is clear that technology as a whole has provided the basis for an ever increasing trend towards individual freedom and has also enabled a move away from the monarchies and traditional houses of power which have controlled and influenced large parts of the world for millenniums.

The move towards blockchain technology as a money on a 50 year time frame is contributing to an 80 year populist uprising against the current power structure that are upholding the current 250 year empire cycle in the post American revolution world.

Are you starting to see how all these cycles are not only lining up but also feeding into each other. Leading to what can potentially be not only a big revolutionary period, but also a move to disable would be power structures that don't provide value to the public for the first time in human history. What a time to be alive.

Touching back on chapter 2, not only are we living through a time where the fiat Ponzi is at a peak, but we are also at a very unique time in history when you zoom out, ready for revolution. Very few people actually notice the zoomed out historical patterns as their world view is totally controlled and manipulated.

Those are the historical cycles and patterns to take into account.

Moving beyond historical cycles and patterns we need to also take into account some other factors such as adoption curves. This goes more into the theory of "gradually then suddenly".

As you can see if the charts below, adoptions of new technologies generally accelerate very rapidly once a technology has been adopted by 5% of people and it becomes evident that those who do adopt the technology are gaining advantage over those who do not. This self-fulfilling incentive structure drives people to adopt the new technology.

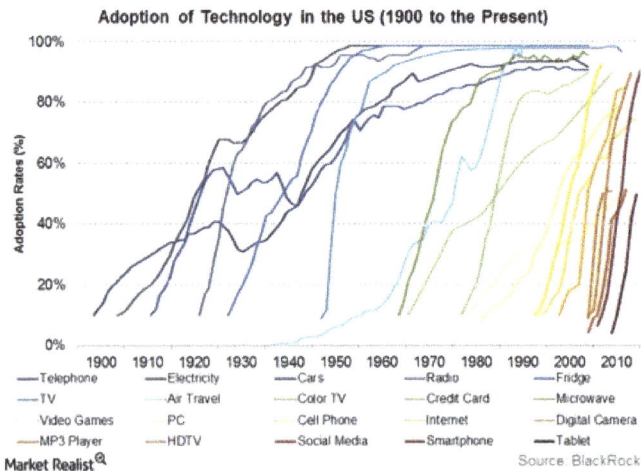

Adoption of Technology in the US (1900 to the Present)

Estimates vary on global crypto adoption however a vast majority of estimates range between 4% - 15%. I use crypto adoption as it shows the % of people searching for alternatives to traditional systems as a whole, whether that be for money itself or smart contract platforms.

With that said, crypto adoption may also not be the best indicator of the technology itself as there are many participants within the industry who are only there to make more dollars. Not for the revolution itself or the benefits that it by its nature can bring.

Below is a chart that illustrates a textbook s-curve adoption process.

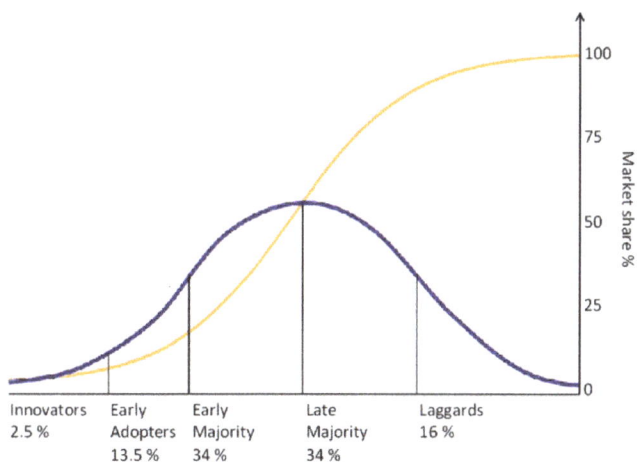

The question is, what is going to drive this adoption process? What benefits are the adopters going to gain over those who don't adopt it?

The answer is simple in one sense and complicated in another. Which segways to the next chapter perfectly.

Chapter 4

Technocracy and Globalism

In understanding the bigger picture from a zoomed out perspective, I think it is hard not to mention the globalist organisations, their openly stated agenda's that they plan to introduce and enforce on the populations of the world, the role that they play on a global level, as well as the ever growing technocracy that is seemingly being implemented with or without them. This is what will largely drive adoption to new technologies as those who adopt them will have a significant advantage in nearly every aspect of life from business to freedom of association over those who don't. Understanding this knowledge now, ahead of time, is what will give you an advantage in identifying opportunities over those who don't.

It is with this knowledge, that we can see which way the globe is trending towards (freedom or oppression). We can also see what forces are going to drive the converging revolution cycles we spoke about last chapter.

Some logical precedents you need to understand this chapter are:

1) Humans are hierarchical animals.
2) Consequently, there is a global hierarchy.
3) And that there has always been a global hierarchy.

Humans are social creatures.

This is not a conspiracy; this is just natural human behaviour playing out over time. Humans are hierarchical animals thus hierarchy's form. Being in a global world today, hierarchies have formed on a global level. This is nothing strange.

These hierarchies have formed in the shape of globalist organisations and globalism in general. As it is by its nature, the most broad and thus powerful hierarchy that can form on planet earth.

Globalism itself, to clarify, is not globalisation. Globalism is the idea of "the operation or planning of economic, social and foreign policy on a global basis." Whereas Globalisation is the process of interaction and integration among people, companies, and governments worldwide. On a decentralized, voluntary basis according to each entities needs and wants.

Key words, "on a global basis".

There are more than a few organisations who we can refer to as "globalist organisations". Often, they have come out and actively promoted some of the Malthusian ideas with regards to policies and agendas that have large effects on the freedoms and rights of everyday people, business' and even over arch national governments policies.

One could and perhaps even should write an entire book about the global power structure today and the history of global power structures that have led us to this point in history.

I will not go into extreme detail of the past 2000 years of global power structures and how they have operated to position themselves above everybody else to implement their self-interests.

Instead, I will focus on today's globalist power structures, what their openly stated agendas are and what their openly stated tools are. So that we can make an opinion about whether the trend will continue or reverse its current direction of decreasing freedom and choice around the world, the factors which would ultimately drive the eventual adoption of Monero globally.

Even with that said, there is a lot of interconnectivity and detail between the players and the layers of the global power structure. However, I will simply include what I think is enough detail to illustrate the point and not the crazy amount of detail one could include.

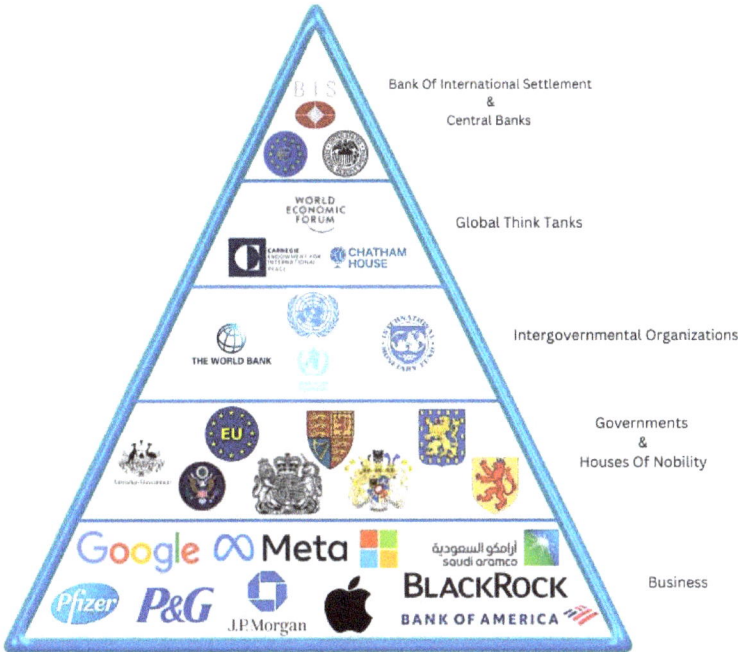

The global power structure today can be broken down relatively simply as illustrated above.

This is not a conspiracy but rather just 100% facts, laid out to show you the power structure that exists according to the evidence and receipts.

The "rabbit holes" into the details spanning centuries regarding the formation of the most powerful power structures really are incredibly deep and nuanced and I would be lying if I said I came even remotely close to understanding it. However, the history of global power certainly affects the world we see today in a very profound way, It's through this deep complexity and opaqueness that they are able to deceive and thrive.

Layer 1:

The Bank of International Settlements (BIS) & Central Banks

The BIS and central banks sit at the top of the hierarchy, regarding power and influence.

The BIS is the oldest and most powerful global bank in the world. Commonly known as the Central Bank of Central Banks. Even by their own terminology, this is what they are called.

The main objective of this bank is upholding and facilitating the functions of central banks and by extension, the fiat system that creates wealth out of thin air (via stealing purchasing power from us) and distributing it as they see fit.

The best resource I have found for a highly comprehensive history and analysis of the BIS is "Tower of Basel" by Adam Lebor. Here however, we will give you a brief overview of the BIS, so as to educate the reader about the threats that the BIS pose to individual sovereignty and ultimately freedom. We have already mentioned central banking at length in Chapter 2, so we will not cover it extensively again.

A Quick History:

The BIS was initially set up post WW1 in 1930 to deal with reparation payments from Germany. The BIS's function was to act as the trustee for the German Governments International Loan (Young Loan) that was floated in 1930, it was however by 1932 that the banks usefulness became obsolete as Reparation payments from Germany were first suspended under the Hoover moratorium in June 1931, and then abolished altogether under the Lausanne Agreement in July of 1932.

The bank became largely obsolete however did not fold, they instead focused on their second main objective, which was defined as "fostering the cooperation between its member central banks". Which is very similar to the terminology that they use today.

Later, the BIS functioned as a neutral intermediary and financed both sides of WW2, they functioned as an off ramp for German gold so the Germans could purchase materials needed and also performed functions for the allies and the Swiss banks who had ties to the allies.

Given this fact, you would think that the bank would some way or another have been buried post WW2. However, this was not to be. During the 1944 Bretton Woods Conference, the "liquidation of the Bank for International Settlements at the earliest possible moment" was recommended. This however resulted in the BIS being a subject of a dispute and disagreement between the U.S. and the UK.

The liquidation of the bank was supported by other European delegates, as well as Americans (including Harry Dexter White and Secretary of the Treasury Henry Morgenthau Jr.). Abolition was opposed by John Maynard Keynes, head of the British delegation, the namesake from which today's global "Keynesian economics" Ponzi is based.

Despite the opposition from J.M Keynes, the next day the abolition was approved, however the abolition of the bank never actually happened.

In April 1945, just before the end of the war in Europe, the new U.S. president Harry S. Truman ended U.S. involvement in the scheme. Following which, the British government suspended the dissolution and then in 1948 the decision to liquidate the BIS was officially reversed.

Post WW2, the bank has really had to find ways to justify its existence. And justify its existence it did.

The bank today, sets many regulations for the entire global financial & banking systems and the 64 (currently) central bank members.

Consequently, it connects the various global central banking cartels into a centralized global organisation. Naturally, the BIS boasts a lot of power, since it has the ability to totally control the flow of money to and from any industry, nation or agendas they see fit. As we know, money is power. Thus, it controls the flow of power according to those who play its game of monetary manipulation.

Fun Fact: The BIS is legally immune from many laws that apply to not only other banks but also us as individuals.

It is through the regulation and monetary control that they are able to excerpt so much influence on the direction of the world, funnel funds to and from where they see fit based on their arbitrarily set goals. The agendas are by nature, based on the ideological agendas of those who are involved with the BIS. At the end of the day, they set the agenda for central banks who in turn, set the agenda for major national economies and global think tanks, who in turn set the agenda for business' and populations, who have no choice but to implement/follow these agendas or risk having their door kicked down.

Believe it or not, in addition to the global regulation they set, the BIS is actually a participant in many markets including the bond market and the precious metals market. This in effect has meant the rigging of many markets due to the sheer size of positions geared in certain directions (a key Keynesian philosophy) as well as the influence via regulation over the entire banking system and thus the movement of money to and from certain assets has been rigged.

As a consequence, they have been able to rig the monetary inflows and outflows of markets & institutions all over the globe from national governments to NGO's that affect all aspects of life. Through the manipulation of price of certain assets like gold to the downside, they are able to increase the purchasing power of the dollar to make it appear stronger and less Ponzi like than it actually is. This is another explanation as to why the purchasing power of the dollar has outperformed the increase in the monetary supply, a concept we spoke about in chapter 2.

I'm sure that many of the readers of this book already know, if you can follow the money, you can find the reasoning for pretty much everything that happens. Humans make decisions, it is not because of some divine reason that things happen the way they happen. Humans make them happen and humans are driven by money and greed. Therefore logically, money is the reasoning for many decisions made.

With that said, the BIS is at the top of all monetary flows meaning that in either a direct or roundabout way, the BIS dictates or at minimum influences/approves inadvertently the decisions and power structures in the world as we see it today.

The members of the BIS (the heads of the world central banks) go to Basel every 2 months to discuss a range of topics which are usually kept very secretive, however considering the people who go there and the purpose of the BIS, we can safely assume they are at minimum talking about how best to control/gear the global economy via the use of fiat money and other mechanisms, it is pretty obvious that they are not talking about the weather.

Now that we have established that the BIS sits at the top of global decision making. Probably the most important thing to note out of this whole subtopic, is the publicly stated agenda's that the BIS is going to or are currently pushing,

The BIS wants to and has stated for numerous years now, their plan to introduce CBDC's aka Central Bank Digital currencies (which we will get more into later in this chapter). Additionally, their interests lie completely in keeping the fiat Ponzi alive... after all they are quite literally only existent with the existence of central banks and by extension, fiat currency.

They have also been highlighting "green finance" aka ESG (environmental & social governance), which is akin to a social credit score of sorts. Bare in mind that they are completely controlling/influencing the direction of money based on agendas that meet criteria set out by the BIS, an unelected intergovernmental organisation that is not beholden to the free market, nor anyone for that matter.

Pure communism. On a global level.

The policies they have openly set are all clear indicators for where the money will inevitably flow to and from.

Below the BIS, you have the central banks of different nations. Briefly, the central banks directly control the monetary systems of their respective nations, ensuring that any agreed upon agenda set through the guise of the BIS can be enforced effectively across many parts of the globe. Certainly all major economies.

Layer 2: Policy Distributors & Global Think Tanks.

The second layer in what functions as the global power structure is the think tanks who act as policy distributors. Most notorious of which is probably the **World Economic Forum (WEF).**

To give you a quick history, The World Economic Forum was founded in 1971 (familiar year, right?) by Klaus Schwab. A name you will come to know well if you don't already.

The WEF is responsible for organising the Davos summit of global leaders each year and has done so since 1988. The Davos summit is a large global summit which most people are familiar with.

The WEF can be grouped in with a bunch of other organisations such as the council on foreign relation, Chatham house & the Carnegie endowment for international peace, who all function as "global think tanks". They write policy papers for nations based on their "research" and find subvert ways to trickle their often dystopian agendas into democracies across the world. They in essence, act as an academic legitimiser to many of the socialist dystopian agendas. Which is a cultural sales tactic to get populations to agree, accept or at minimum get them to not care enough to stand up against it.

To give a brief overview of the WEF, sitting on the board of trustees is very important and prominent people. Kristalina Georgieva (Managing Director of the IMF), prominent central bankers, leaders from some of the biggest Silicon Valley tech companies, Larry Fink of BlackRock, Al Gore, Christine Lagarde (Head of the ECB), leaders from the global business world and even government ministers from various governments around the world.

Over time these exact people will change however what will remain constant is the appointment of people of tremendous global power and their ability to influence government policy around the world to implement their agendas. Often socialist, freedom depriving agendas. Its very hard to argue that with such "penetration", as Klaus likes to say, that their agendas will go unnoticed.

The mission of the WEF as per the WEF is "improving the state of the world by engaging business, political, academic, and other leaders of society to shape global, regional, and industry agendas".

In other words, for those of you who are already aware, they advocate the best way to achieve these goals is through "public/private partnerships". Which is just another way of saying "communism".

The organisation is funded by its 1,000 members which are some of the most powerful and influential companies and individuals in the world, believe it or not, one of the members is King Charles III

Sounds innocent enough, right?

To get to the point rather quickly, to fill you in as the reader. One of the WEF's major agendas is something coined as "The Great Reset".

I am trying to write this from a rather unbiased point of view as to just simply show you the facts, however the agendas in the great reset are for the most part, nothing short of completely psychopathic and evil in my view.

It is factual to say that the agendas they are pushing are socialist agendas and also increase the amount of power held by the current global power structure to a point where they control or significantly influence a vast majority of the world's infrastructure & resources as well as going so far as infringing on the basic rights and autonomy of an individual's freedoms and choices.

Therefore, it is factual to say that they are advocating for a global communist agenda and have great ability to implement these unelected, unprofitable and unpopular communist agendas in sly roundabout ways.

Notoriously, the great reset publicly advocates for some of the following policies:

- CBDC's
- Digital ID's
- Carbon credit scores
- Equality of outcome
- A Ban on beef and other "non-environmentally friendly" foods
- Eat bugs... No, I am not joking.
- And the famous "You'll own nothing. and you'll be happy".

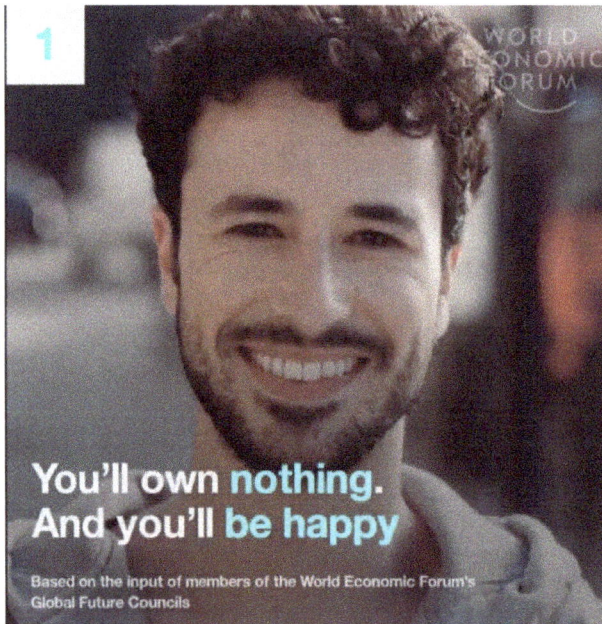

The overall goals they espouse are not necessarily bad, I mean, who would proactively want to destroy the earth? Or Who would proactively want discrimination and inequality? Or who would want crime to be rife within a society?

It is the means they use to achieve them which are inherently psychopathic and evil. They use these goals that every single normal person naturally wants and frames the only solution as over reaching dystopian agendas.

I won't go into extreme detail as you can research more at your own pace. I simply write this to inform the reader. It is up to you how far you want to dive down the WEF rabbit hole, I don't want to shove it down your throats. Klaus Schwab has written numerous books about the socialist agenda that he and the WEF are trying to install around the world.

Frankly, if I did go into all the detail, you would not believe me and you would likely call me a conspiracy theorist, which really says a lot about how crazy his ideas and agendas are. The reality is that Klaus Schwab has written all of these agendas in his books, and it is evident in WEF policy & agendas that they try to promote. For those curious, the books are:

1) The Fourth Industrial Revolution, (2016). ISBN 978-1944835002.
2) Shaping the Future of the Fourth Industrial Revolution, (2018).
3) COVID-19: The Great Reset, (2020). ISBN 978-2940631124.
4) Stakeholder Capitalism: A Global Economy that Works for Progress, People and Planet. (2021). ISBN 1119756138, 978-1119756132.
5) The Great Narrative: For a Better Future, (2022). ISBN 978-2940631315.

The point here is the fact that the WEF holds the largest annual gathering of world leaders who have the ability to implement these agendas in many ways, shapes and forms. As well as directly employing many global leaders from many fields from business to politics.

Do you think this will have no impact going forward? Especially considering the fact that we have seen their agendas increasingly creep into our society.

Look around you, what world do you observe? Do you observe a world with growing freedom and prosperity or do you observe a world in which socialist clown world agendas that nobody voted for are being implemented and the individual is losing freedom, wealth and prosperity?

Based on the observations of the direction of the world, our ever-diminishing freedoms and the ever-increasing socialist measures being implemented, I believe this trend has no reason to change thus will not or perhaps cannot change without significant reform of the areas which keep them in power i.e. The monetary system.

Actions and legislation that can only be sustained by the ability of the fiat system to create money out of thin air is what is keeping them in place. Thus, you can see how they are linked.

The other institutions mentioned such as Chatham house, Carnegie endowment for international peace etc can all be lumped together with the WEF for agendas that they want to implement and actions that they take to install their agenda's. As mentioned, it's a deep hole to explore, so feel free to go down the full extent of it once you have finished reading this book.

Layer 3:

Next up is the IMF, The International Monetary Fund. World Bank. USAID etc

The IMF brings countries under the order of the global agenda via money and the financial system, in short. The IMF, The World Bank, USAID etc, are able to lure nations into towing the global agendas (often US or globalist led) via "development lending" or "donations".

The IMF, World Bank & USAID will only lend to and "help" nations who implement many of the global laws surrounding many aspects from currency exchange to Drug legislation to COVID lockdown/mask/vaccine regulations. Basically, they only help countries who toe the line.

There is a clear trend that the IMF will continue to be used as a tool by the UN and other global organisations to implement the prescribed agenda Likewise will the World Bank and USAID by their respective counterparts. Since the global development agenda is becoming more socialist, I think it is a reasonable expectation that they will continue to be used as a tool to implement these agendas on various national levels, such as we have already seen.

Like the IMF, **The World Bank** provides monetary assistance to countries.

According to the world bank website they "provide low-interest loans, zero to low-interest credits, and grants to developing countries. These support a wide array of investments in such areas as education, health, public administration, infrastructure, financial and private sector development, agriculture, and environmental and natural resource management.". These loans come from some of the freshest dollars printed.

They also only provide loans to nations who implement laws and agendas of multinational organisations and the US led global power agenda. For example, COVID regulations.

The point here is not that its good or bad but rather how easy it is to bully nations (especially developing nations) into implementing laws that serve no benefit to the people of the country. This is factually known to currently be in existence. And you can see their ability to influence the world with access to the money printer to then dangle a carrot in front of many nations. Again, without control of the monetary spigot

THE UN and their arms i.e., WHO, Security council, ICC etc

Like many of the UN arms, the WHO is used to implement policy based on health. The covid pandemic is a good example of how much power the WHO and these UN organisations can wield based on not much except for arbitrary decisions based on values with either deliberate or accidental misinformation.

To come round full circle with this, Governments, WHO and many organisations around the world like the CDC will give funding to "studies" based on what they are likely to find, then the "scientists" will base their outcomes on what has been paid for. For example, a study about something like "the effects of drugs" is unlikely to come to a conclusion that drugs should be legalized, likewise, a study about "the effects of COVID" is unlikely to come to a result that people should take responsibility for their own life. A scary precedent for dictating global policy is when these types of tools are used to push any agenda, whether you agree with it or not. Putting so called contentious opinions aside such as COVID, this has been a signature move of these organisations in regards to drug policy for the last 50 years and many regulations regarding "safety".

Moving down to layer 4: Governments and Houses of Nobility

Governments and houses of nobility such as Kings, Queens, Lords etc really are a lot further down the power hierarchy than most people would like/care to think. As we have laid out, the policy that most of the world has adopted until this point has been formulated much higher up the hierarchy.

Governments for the most part, serve the function of localised enforcement and spruiking of the agendas set on the higher levels.

As we often see, many members of parliament and houses of nobility also serve on the boards of trustees for many of these NGO's and global think tanks, also intertwining with global business leaders who similarly have the position with the NGOs to promote their self-serving agendas and those of their companies.

The members of government are so intertwined with the other layers of the global power hierarchy that the government itself fails its original function of representing the people, which is obviously the illusion they want to portray. Government has becomes intertwined with every level of the global power pyramid from the central banks all the way down to business, politicians almost always have some sort of background within some previous field and or are donated to by people in this field meaning that the level of interconnectivity between these layers and government is very high.

These structures have ultimately led to a situation where a very small group of people from Business, "Philanthropy", government, nobility and other areas are all intertwined and have created establishments that cement their power over many of the democratic and freedom loving processes.

None of this is a conspiracy, it is all 100% fact.

Considering that the global elites at the top of the power pyramid, have all laid out the same agendas, upon which they have their enforcement arms further down the power structure to enforce them, who have also said that they are the agendas they want to implement. Why will we not see these agendas implemented?

When determining the direction of the world based on these global institutions who have a large amount of power, influence and resources, "if it looks like shit and smells like shit, what is it?"

Let me be clear, not every single thing these organisations do is bad or oppressive of freedom. The point is to illustrate the immense amount of power that these global organisations hold, the interconnectivity of the elites who run them, the agendas they have openly stated that they want to implement and how they can and have been used to implement agendas on a global level.

When we look at the connectivity between The BIS and other central banks, Global think tanks, Global business, governments, houses of nobility and enforcers such as the IMF & world bank. It is clear to see that a vast majority of the worlds power structure, and processes in regards to how agendas are implemented are not democratically formed and additionally, they are very centralized between a relatively small group of people with a very high amount of interconnectivity that all want the same agendas.

Layer 5:

The layer of big business need not be mentioned in great extent as many of the characters in charge of big business are intertwined within governments, Think Tanks and basically all the levels of the power pyramid illustrated earlier. If they are not currently in control of business, they have almost always had successful careers within business, finance and/or banking and have left their positions for positions closer to the money spigot.

Businesses are often used by the higher level up the pyramid as an enforcement layer for their agendas. As an example, funding/loans are only made available to companies that comply with ESG (Environmental, social, and governance) or DEI (Diversity, equity, and inclusion) mandates. Whether or not they ideologically agree with the mandates, they are forced to comply with the mandates in order to gain funding which when you boil it down, helps to grow, expand and ultimately complete. Therefore, they are forced to follow socialist policies and agendas in order to compete in a market. Therefore when you boil it down even further, its socialism or economic death. A simple choice for any business person with legal obligations to do there best for the company.

Given that the consumer is largely unaware of policies like this (potentially on purpose), it is impossible for consumers to spend their money with companies they ideologically agree with or with companies who support the world they want to see, instead it has all been made to appear uniform.

All in all, this small group of business', who control a large amount of the world's resources and influence, are often forced to support given agendas in order to receive funding.

They all, however, are pushing agendas that infringe severely on the rights and freedoms of the everyday person and do nothing but serve to increase the centralization in control over resources and influence.

Given this and the fact that we see how decisions are implemented on a global level, it's clear to see the direction in which the world will be heading.

An important mention for layer 5 players that are being used as a weapon against freedom and prosperity is firstly Blackrock, an investment company/asset manager that is run by none other than WEF board of trustees member, Larry Fink.

Blackrock has 10 trillion dollars' worth of assets under management. Which for those unaware, is a lot of money. A lot of the 10 trillion dollars of assets comes from people like You and I, people with 401K, superannuation, or pension funds.

How BlackRock is used to implement the agendas set higher is through what they choose to fund and not to fund, which is almost always, non-business related criteria such as ESG and now DEI as well. That is not only startups but massive fortune 500 companies too. As Larry Fink says "You have to force behaviours" and "We're going to have to force change". Yes, that means they will only invest in companies that neglect their prime fiduciary responsibility to look after their shareholders in favour of "social justice". In other words, BlackRock withholds money from companies and industries that don't support the woke agenda of 729 genders, equality of outcome, hiring based on race & gender.

What do you think companies will do when their ability to exist or compete is based on whether or not they can virtue signal. Of course, they will virtue signal and implement woke policies throughout their corporation.

Similarly, companies such as Google are used in the sense that they are at time forced to prioritize search results that are in accordance with the agenda, also known as "the science" during the COVID pandemic. It was impossible to find literally anything that didn't support mandatory masks, mandatory lockdowns, "The vax is good and has no side effects" blah blah and an all-round attack on anyone who didn't militantly and unquestionably support these agendas, it was essentially illegal to say people should take responsibility for the consequences in their life or that people should be free to make their own choices. Similarly, try and find documents about the Hunter Biden laptop etc, its almost impossible now let alone in 2020 when the CIA was used to tell big tech companies to block/deprioritize articles/users talking about it etc, as it was "Russian misinformation". We know this is true because of the "twitter files", which were released by Elon Musk after his takeover of Twitter in 2022.

We also know, due to the Twitter files, that departments from every corner of the government from CIA, FBI, DHS, DOD, HHS, Global Engagement Centre etc had direct access to Twitter to make "moderation requests" of people or content that should be de-amplified or blocked. Similarly, at least 20 quasi-entities (mostly partially or fully funded by government grants) who had the same privilege.

We also see that PayPal has notoriously implemented a policy that allows them to fine you $2000 for saying things that they disagree with on social media. Similarly, GoFundMe has been forced by governments to shut down funding to agendas that they don't like.

Additionally, "Mainstream Media" or "Legacy Media" as I call it, is nothing more than a paid for instrument to control the thoughts and standards for cultural acceptability of the masses, never more evident than during the COVID Pandemic. In case you didn't know, you can literally pay to have things broadcast.

We can see through all these examples, plus the Hundreds more that I didn't mention, that corporations & big business around the world in all sectors have been, at best, corrupted by the agendas set above and are used as various tools for implementing specified agendas.

Moving forward, before the fiat Ponzi dies, these globalists organisations from the BIS, to the WEF etc, still have many cards left to play in order to keep alive the system that keeps them artificially at the top. They will go to extreme lengths to keep their position, as most people who have become extremely deluded by their sense of grandiosity would, to be fair.

I think it is important to note that while many of these tools highlighted earlier such as CBDC's, Social/Carbon Credit Scores etc are not only openly discussed as agendas by those who control the spigot, but also anecdotally, we can clearly see that the world is becoming more and more digital every day and that solutions to many analogue systems we have today, will be digital. Digital solutions will also be sought in areas which there are no current solutions. Such is the habit of human behaviour.

Not only digital, but we also see that the world is becoming increasingly "less free". So, to implement these tools would not be going against the general trend of the world/ causing a revolution. It would simply be a continuation of the previous policies that they have influenced whilst continuing to be at the top of the power structure.

Considering money is influence and the power structure's ability to implement their agenda's, you would have to be rather mentally questionable to disagree that these will inevitably happen considering that the entire global power structure is all more or less, pushing for the same agenda, as we have mentioned.

These tools/technologies essentially equate to weapons to achieve their goal of prolonging the current global power structure as long as possible, using fiat to financially prop it up.

The tools that will be used to continue the trends of less freedom, increasing encroachment on personal privacy and the ever increasing centralization of global power are:

CBDC's or Central Bank Digital Currencies.

Central bank digital currencies are currencies issued by a central bank similar to what we see today with fiat however without a physical cash version available. Basically, just numbers on a screen, to dumb it down. Numbers on a screen with a twist. And that twist is that for the first time in history, the money they give us is completely programmable.

This leaves us with 0 autonomy from the government and their set agendas, in regard to financial freedom. If you cannot spend your money at your own free will, then what can you do?

For example, if you want to go protest for literally anything besides approved protests, then the government will see on social media through your digital ID and KYC internet (we discuss this more later in the chapter) that you have taken interest in going and won't approve your transaction to put fuel in your car or purchase of a public transport ticket. Obviously, then you cannot go, and as such, all your actions require government approval. Pretty good system, right?

It may sound extreme buts that's ultimately the level of control that these tools provide.

As a civilization, we become completely under the control and approval of whoever is making/influencing the laws of the day. This presents a severe probability of the population becoming nothing more than easily moveable pawns to politicians seeking to implement their agenda, in other words, that's you and I. Maybe you think it's a good idea because you agree with the set agendas, well, would it still be a good idea if "the opposite party" was in power. If your answer is no, then you should be wholeheartedly against this technology since it will happen one day, that's a foregone conclusion.

Having someone or a small group of people with this tremendous amount of power over everyone can never end well. Historically speaking, a situation where someone has complete control over a population has never ended well.

Looking at China, we can see a good blueprint of what can and/or will be rolled out with the use of a CBDC.

CBDC's have been the absolute death of freedom and choice in China where implemented.

But it would never happen here, right?

Well, CBDC's are in the process of being developed by many western countries around the world. Including USA, Australia and many parts of Europe. According to the governments, this is to "modernize" payment system and increase efficiency in payments across the economy.

To me it seems obvious that they will usher in CBDC's under the guise of safety and efficiency... like they did in China. Like they do for every dystopian policy in every dystopian regime ever. In fact, their advertisements for the CBDC based payment systems already include safety and efficiency as key selling points for their programs that diminish our freedoms.

The narrative will likely include "efficiency", "safety", "anti-terrorism", "anti-money laundering" and add this on top of any more localised narrative of the day such as "cash transmits covid" or "we need to implement CBDC's to save the environment from nasty PoW coins" (likely Bitcoin will be the scapegoat). It doesn't actually matter what the exact narrative is, we will see that the underlying themes remain the same.

Since cash is already dying, it won't take much of a narrative shift or minor justification to put the final nail in the coffin of cash, which from a fiat sense is the last bastion of any semblance of freedom.

Nearly the entire public besides the remnant will blindly accept this or at least not care enough to do anything about it... They will say to themselves "We already pretty much transact through our bank cards i.e., digital money, so what does it matter?"

Little do they know; this will be the death of freedom.

Eventually, tied to their digital ID and social credit score.

The truth behind all of this is that the fiat Ponzi is crashing, the power establishment propped up because of fiat is losing their grip over the world, the economy is crashing (the market is rising but real economic indicators are woeful) and frankly, they will need to do something about it.

CBDC's can and most likely will (over a long enough period of time) be used to incentivise certain economic behaviours to control economic activity such as:

- **Time limits** on your money i.e., you have to spend your money before a certain time otherwise you lose it. This is already happening in China. This would likely be to increase velocity of money, increase spending, increase tax receipts etc, all important economic indicators. This can also come in the form of negative interest rates.

- **Spending will be limited to certain areas,** or portions of income will be allotted to specific items. The reasoning behind this would be growth of those industries and overall GDP, most likely popular and nationally important industries, as 2 examples of financial controls that will likely be introduced.

In this specific case, it would all be in an attempt to paint the picture and manipulate the economic stats for the benefits of the political narrative of the day BUT at the cost of any semblance of freedom.

They will likely shape the narrative of CBDC's as being similar to Monero/Bitcoin however an important distinction that nearly every single normie will overlook is the difference between DLT (distributed ledger technology) and decentralised blockchains run by nodes... after all, who can expect a normie to understand the difference and total nuance of it all. They sound sort of similar, right?

This sly and deceptive distinction will allow them to roll in their DLT based CBDC with 1 node... The federal reserve/Reserve bank of the relevant country.

The only solution to CBDC's and the end of freedom as we know it, are cryptocurrencies.

Digital ID's

Digital IDs are a pretty simple idea, which to be fair, almost seem like an inevitable outcome in an increasingly digital society.

The theory is that a good digital ID system could unlock new possibilities in the economic, social, and political realms. Theoretically, a digital ID system would provide verification and authentication to a high degree of assurance and uniqueness with protection of the user privacy, and control over personal data.

Digital IDs are simply a digital version of the analogue Identification systems we use in society today. Sounds okay, right?

Despite the possible tangible benefits from a digital ID system, digital ID's still present a significant risk of their own, that require proper controls. To start with, as with any over centralized control system whose motivations are not compatible with any or all users, there is the severe potential for misuse, certainly given a long enough time period.

Digital Identification technologies, like so many other technologies in society, can be known as "dual use" technologies. Other examples of such technologies are social media, GPS, or even nuclear energy. A technology that can be used both to benefit society in a potentially game changing way and conversely can also be used for undesirable purposes by governments, institutions, or individual actors. In fact, most, if not all technologies are "dual use".

History provides us with countless unsavoury examples of misuse of identification programs or their own programs in general, including tracking or persecuting ethnic and religious groups.

If designed poorly or without proper controls (which seems likely with any experimental technology or any technology with centralized control), digital ID systems could easily be used in ways that target the interests of individuals or groups by governments or even by the private sector.

To guard against such misuse. Individual consent, protection of user privacy and control over personal data components are critical. Individual consent does not include "accept the terms or you cannot participate in society", that is blackmail.

Is this really a probable outcome though? Do we believe there will be an option for participation free of coercion?

And if so, do we believe they will be used for an everlasting period of time, in ways that don't target or manipulate certain individuals or groups who don't tow the agenda of the day?

Certainly from a historical perspective, the % chance of that happening is 0%.

So, let's talk about some of the potential ramifications and things that could go wrong.

- **Vaccine passports:** If anything has become apparent with what we saw during the COVID hysteria period was that governments and business' will jump at the idea of restricting many areas of your life completely arbitrarily and in addition, will use technological means by which to increase your compliance with the mainstream agenda. In this case, QR codes to track and limit movements, propaganda on legacy media and censorship of alternative media/individuals who do not share the same values as the narrative.

This is not a rant about COVID but rather when you think about it, the option to lockdown and restrict movement is nothing more than opinion. The establishment guises it as a fact under "it's the science" however common sense will tell you that there is more than 1 qualitative or quantitative indicator to take into account when making any given decision relating to anything in this world.

To say it is a fact that we need to lockdown is the same as saying we need to lockdown to prevent people getting hit by buses. Technically yes, it will reduce the number of people being hit by buses, but we know that this would be a silly solution as there is more than 1 indicator to take into account. COVID restrictions are no different.

The point here is that we saw crazy restrictions in many parts of the world that were introduced in the propaganda fuelled hysteria that was a vast majority of the COVID pandemic.

Now imagine a scenario, imagine if there were vaccine passports tied to your Digital ID meaning that if you wanted to go to places such as a supermarket or a restaurant, you would need to scan your Digital ID which had your vaccine passport connected to it.

This kind of system is rife for misuse. The amount of power that becomes centralized into the hands of a few is historically speaking, a very dangerous path to be walking.

- **A way to collect all of your biometric data**. Such as facial and retinal scans as well as fingerprints. This can easy be disguised as "if you have done nothing wrong, then you have nothing to worry about". However, our biometric data and bodily autonomy are really at the core of what freedom is. Owning the data about the very essence of what we are made of is essential to any free society. If we ourselves, as individuals do not own our own data, then really what do we own? Certainly, we can say that there is no freedom if the options are be excluded from society or forfeit your bodily data

Additionally, as a societal precedent, being guilty until proven innocent is not the way any prosperous society has run in the past, nor can it by its own merit be a way in which a prosperous society can run. Only authoritarian regimes that benefit the 0.01% have implemented such logical precedents into their societies.

- **A way to track your every move.** Tracking your movements between buildings/venues like during covid with the QR scanners. Tracking where you move to due to restrictions associated your social credit score, but we will get more into that in the next section. Needless to say, the potential dangers and opportunities for misuse here are massive and also grave. This would naturally provide a great platform for a digital prison or panopticon.

Now imagine that all of this data was to be hacked and open to the public forever, would that still make you feel safe? We have seen government systems be hacked countless times. The government is not and nor should they ever be a technology or cyber security company... they don't even function successfully in their current role let alone to expand their role to something that they have even less idea about.

Governments around the world are framing the adoption of digital IDs with all too common dystopian buzzwords such as "safe", "efficient" & "convenient" to name a few.

Digital IDs are already starting to be rolled out in various places, a few examples are digital driving licenses and digital ID systems associated with social security/government services.

I just like to clarify the point that digital IDs by themselves are not anything of any particular major concern, pretty much like any technology or tool. But like with any tool or technology, use cases can be warped and essentially switched from productive to the many to harmful for the many.

Before we move onto social credit scores, just think about how the tool could potentially be misused by those seeking to implement them as part of a broader agenda, say an agenda that could be used against you, used against the best interest of your life and then how damaging this tool could be when used incorrectly as part of a broader plan incorporating different tools. A way of thinking which I think is productive to examine whether any measure will have a positive impact or not (especially when we are talking about legislation), is how could the legislation be used to impact you if your worst enemy was implementing/enforcing it.

The conclusion I come to in this case, is that Digital ID's can be one of the most damaging linchpins that underlies a digital panopticon.

Social credit scores

Digital ID's and CBDC's are the basis under which effective social credit systems can be implemented.

For those unaware, social credit scores are point systems designed by governments that award and deduct points to and from people based on many aspects of a person's life from behaviour in public (which is monitored with facial recognition surveillance everywhere tied to your Digital ID or through designated "information collectors" aka paid snitches, like we see in China) to financial transactions. Based on whether the actions are encouraged or discouraged by the government, a new tiered rights system is awarded to the person.

Broken down simply, A social credit system is a score based on your CBDC tied to your Digital ID. As well as the "monitoring" of your behaviour in pubic, this includes social media.

As we see in China right now, some of the rewards and punishments within a social credit system can be:

Potential Rewards:

- Lower utility costs
- Lower rent
- Access to higher quality medical treatment
- Lower Interest rates for loans
- Being able to rent bikes/cars etc without a deposit.
- Tax Breaks

Potential Punishments:

- No access to transport.
- Restricted Transport methods i.e., Banned travelling via plane or fast trains.
- No access to high end products.
- Access to lower quality or no medical care.
- Public shaming.
- "Re-education" Camp.
- No/Restricted access to financial services.
- Personal information made openly available to society.

On the face value of a social credit score to reward good behaviour and punish bad behaviour, it may seem like a good or progressive idea. After all, who doesn't want to live in a safe prosperous society? But therein lies the danger, what is safe? And what is prosperous? 2 definitions completely left open for interpretation in many areas of everyday life. Each person would have a different answer to those questions.

The door is left wide open for a complete digital panopticon where all aspects of life can be controlled and assessed. Not only is it left wide open, its in fact designed solely for that purpose.

Looking at China for one example, if you cross the road while the crossing light is red, it has a warning that comes over the loudspeaker, saying "you are crossing illegally, turn back now" and then deducts points from your social credit score for "endangering yourself and others" around you. This is due to the fact that the facial recognition cameras are linked to the digital ID system which allows the camera to determine who is committing the offence, btw the facial recognition systems are good enough to identify you even whilst wearing a mask. Sounds like paradise, right?

This is only one example, and it may seem irrelevant, however, I have used this example as it shows a use case so miniscule that it goes to show that if they will apply it to circumstances like these, then what else will they apply it to? After all, who doesn't want to be safe?

As mentioned, what one does on social media or WeChat is also assessed and scored by the social credit score system. If one is to talk in a negative light about President Xi or the CCP (Chinese Communist Party), there score is respectively deducted.

If one buys too much alcohol there score is deducted as it shows "irresponsible behaviour" and lord knows we don't want a society full of "irresponsible" people. Similarly, buying baby formula if you have a baby is viewed in a positive light as "responsible behaviour".

Believe it or not, the CCP even goes are far as tracking people via their phones connected to their digital ID's to see if people are visiting their elderly parents or grandparents enough, as this is a "good Chinese value". Just for the record, I'm not joking.

One could in fact write an entire chapter or book about dystopia in China with the use of these "technologies", but I feel it would be counter-productive to continue writing about it in this book.

The real point is that a system like this can very easily be used to control every aspect of your life and implement an agenda that is not part of your moral philosophy.

Ask yourself again, if your worst enemy got a hold of this system, would you feel comfortable? If the answer is no, then you should be against any type of system such as this one or the ones previously mentioned. Contrary to this, would it not be better where we can all pursue what is in accordance with our moral philosophy and peacefully respect others who want to pursue something different. After all, what someone else does, does not affect you.

A social credit score can also very sneakily, come in the form of a "Carbon Credit Score", which gives and takes rights to consumers like you and I, based on the "eco-friendliness" of our purchases and actions. Essentially, an ESG and DEI score for the everyday person. The WEF has already announced at the Davos conference (a conference of all global leaders) that they are working on a Carbon Credit Score system.

A system like this would include a carbon credit allowance on your purchases. This would mean that once you hit a certain level of "carbon" associated with each purchase you make, your bankcard/CBDC money would stop working until the next period in which your carbon allowance renews.

To give an example, meat purchases, specifically steak/beef would be allotted a high carbon score meaning that it would not be possible to purchase it on a regular basis and therefore you would be forced to buy other products which have been allotted a lower carbon score such as bugs for example. Don't call me a conspiracy theorist just yet if this concept is new to you.

Similarly, flights and other types of travel and freedom can be severely limited as they could be allotted a high carbon score.

With many of the carbon credit systems blueprinted, there has almost exclusively been carbon trading schemes associated with the design which ultimately leaves the door open for more control over the majority of the population whilst the rich and ultra-rich can continue to do as they please as the newly imposed costs only allow them to afford it and monopolise the access to goods and services.

This is also true with many resources in general, it allows a small minority of people to have access to and thus control many forms of goods and services. Usually, the mega wealthy and the characters in the globalist organisation.

In any form, all social credit systems come with the inherent serious risk of infringing on even the most basic of human rights such as freedom of choice and we see that it relies on technology that keeps us locked within a digital panopticon. At the control and mercy of whoever is making the decisions on the day and for whatever agenda they are trying to push.

And as we discussed, we know who is in charge and we know what agendas they are trying to implement. Is this the world you want to see?

Like in China, it will also not take long for activities like protesting against the government to be determined as a "danger to society" and thus access to even your own money will be cut off. Leaving you with no choice but to comply with the political narrative of the day endlessly and unquestionably.

Again, I ask, would you trust this amount of power in the hands of your worst enemy?

There is no shadow of doubt within my mind, that the implementation of these systems will lead to the complete end of freedom over an extended period of time, if not immediately. Meaning, people will inherently be driven to search for alternative systems.

A Social credit score will be linked to your Digital ID, which will be linked your CBDC to determine what you can purchase, what you can do etc. The tools for a digital dystopia.

All roads lead to privacy. To me it appears apparently obvious that the future of freedom technologies, namely cryptocurrencies, ABSOLUTELY MUST include privacy technologies to avoid all of these previous problems from CBDC's to Klaus's wet dream of owning nothing and being happy.

Not only from a security and longevity point of view when talking about the pushback against those who are going to be "domestic terrorists" so to say, by purchasing their meat with cryptocurrencies. Also just thinking about average joe moving over to crypto's, naturally, they are not going to want all their finances and financial history to be publicly available for everyone to see for the entirety of human history... they're just not. In the same way that they don't want others to see their bank balances and entire financial lives at the moment. It's just human nature to be private about subjects that can be seen as embarrassing.

This is where Monero comes in.

Without privacy by default, THERE IS NO PRIVACY and without privacy everything is totally censorable... including your purchase of meat. Hence why Bitcoin is not a viable option for long term freedom and prosperity.

All of the systems mentioned earlier in the chapter, claim to be private, they claim to protect the anonymity of users and minimize data requirements sent to other users in the network. This may be partially true, however a way to describe this theory, is that it protects your data horizontally i.e., between users of the network however doesn't protect your data vertically as now the central banks, governments and all institutions of authority have everyone's data surrounding every aspect of their life. A dangerous precedent.

The reason I have not mentioned "Mass surveillance" here in this section of the chapter is because the technologies mentioned thus far, act as a mass surveillance system within itself that give total surveillance and control over a population. Far more effective than a few CCTV cameras.

The point of this chapter was not to go all "tin foil hat conspiracy theorist" on you but rather to fill you in on the details to answer the question from chapter 3 "what is going to drive people to adopt a new technology".

This is it. The dystopian world that is openly stated to be a goal of the "institutions of power"

People will be FORCED to search for alternatives that better suit their needs to achieve the goals that they want to achieve in life and to live the life they want to live. Not to live a life that the globalists want them to live or a life that is/will be forced upon them. That is what slavery is.

At the end of the day, these globalist measures are only possible with a fiat standard because of the ability to prop up these types of unprofitable systems by printing fake money out of thin air to fund them. This segways us to our next few chapters perfectly...

Chapter 5

*PoW & Privacy as **THE** principle for money*

"I don't believe we shall ever have a good money again before we take the thing out of the hands of government, we can't take it violently out of the hands of government, all we can do is by some sly roundabout way introduce something that they can't stop" - Hayek.

So far, we have covered the history of money & the fiat Ponzi. The problems from which have been laid out. Being, fake money that steals value at an exponential rate.

We also have seen the inevitable revolutionary cycles that are set to play out and the reasons which will drive them, being technocracy, globalism, global socialism and the constant attack upon our freedoms and prosperity. With their weapons openly stated in being the introduction of CBDC's, Social Credit scores and digital ID's.

So how do we counter this? How do we lay to bed the bugaboo of all these fiat top signals?

We need to look at the principles required in any technology to solve the problems, once and for all.

1) Fiat = PoW Money (Hard Money)
2) Globalism = Destruction of the money spigot via PoW money (Hard Money) + Private transactions
3) CBDC's, Social Credit Scores, Digital ID's and other attack vectors upon a long lasting basis for freedom and prosperity = Private transactions

Put simply, the 2 principles required for a long lasting platform of freedom and prosperity are PoW and Privacy.

Let's discuss further. I also want to expand on other benefits that 99.9% of the population would never have thought possible, simply by fixing the money.

So, what does PoW solve?

PoW as we discussed is the principle of having limiting factors in the creation of money. Once more, the limiting factor in any successful money has been its ability to be scarce with the reason being that there is work required in making/discovering more.

Philosophically speaking, these are the reasons why money is "work". Money is proof of having done the work. Since the amount of work doable is limited, resources are limited etc, this limits how much "money" can be created.

The value of money is determined by its supply, its supply is limited by how hard money is to create and how hard it is to make is determined by how much work is required to produce more. If something was easy to obtain, for example, it was as easy as pressing a button to obtain, then everyone would create it into oblivion, thus diluting the value of it significantly based on basic supply and demand principles.

However, with gold as an example, since expertise, tools and time are required to increase the supply, we see that a vast majority of people are not willing to/cannot do the work required, it is a lot harder to create (discover) more gold than it is to print money.

Only under these circumstances can money be considered valuable. To refresh, if you can print money out of thin air, it is a direct violation of these PoW principles and hence why it will not be considered valuable by the market... because with the lack of work required to produce it, it becomes abundant. Thus, supply meets demand at a much lower price in a free market.

This importantly, is why coins like Ethereum, Solana or <Insert other shitcoin> can't be used as money. Because they are a replication of the current fiat model on the blockchain, through pre-mining (creating tokens out of thin air, at the inception of the protocol) or through Proof of stake governance, where the more money you have, the more influence you have over the governance of the system.

Proof of work is the only model on which hard money can be based, whether that's gold, Bitcoin or Monero.

From a global power structure sense, this destroys the BIS, central banks and all entities further down the hierarchy that rely on the ability to control monetary policy, such as global think tanks, unproductive government/nobility as well as destroys the ability to funnel money to big business through favourable policy or credit facilities used to implement the agendas on consumers. Boy oh boy, that's a big change.

Having money and monetary policy that is inherently not controlled and inevitably manipulated by anyone, changes the way society works on a much higher level than most people care to think.

Firstly, having a money that doesn't arbitrarily debase encourages people to save, and it actually rewards savings, productivity and responsible allocation of capital that is designed for long term value creation. This is an incredibly important characteristic of a productive and prosperous society that is missing in our current global society. Our society is missing an effective savings technology.

As we see today, the action of saving is punished in the form of inflation/debasement. This means that spending is covertly encouraged as if someone tries to save, they lose their money. This in turn diminishes the important economic health indicator of savings (how much money people have)

On a deeper philosophical level, the move to a hard, "unfuckable" and sound money moves the collective of individuals we call society/civilization to a "low time preference" mind set, instead of the "high time preference" mentality.

Ultimately, the difference between the 2 can be summed up quite simply, high time preference thinking is what we see today in society, where everyone is basically trying to get rich quickly and are also spending on meaningless consumption items at a rate higher than ever in history before. This can really be personified at the peak of illogical activities with the trading of worthless JPEGs for tens of millions of dollars (I know blockchain bros... "it's on the blockchain").

I could give countless examples within and outside the crypto world. From a psychological point of view, many of these behaviours can be traced back to the fact that saving in dollar as has traditionally been the case is a mathematically terrible strategy to gaining wealth, and to act economically rational via savings is not only discouraged but punished.

Low time preference is the ability to act rationally, since you are able to plan out things with much more predictability over longer period of time. You are also able to achieve more things over time.

Moving away from fiat means we can have a low time preference mentality, which, ultimately skews the probability of rational decision of society on all levels and areas.

There are many benefits that many people don't even think of, such as social benefits, environmental benefits and changes would even flow into politics for example.

I want to take this time to be thorough in my approach and inform the reader about the many unforeseen benefits of choosing a non debaseable money, benefits in many areas of society that have probably never even considered before by a broad scale of people. Low time preferences brought about by the move to a PoW money.

Equality of Opportunity & Social Mobility

Throughout human history, the lack of opportunity and social mobility has been one of the most persistent problems that hasn't had a cure… that is, until now.

These same systems of oppression have traditionally been developed from something known as caste systems, which are hereditary power structures.

Inequality CANNOT be a problem when you have genuine social mobility within a society. The only way inequality of outcome can arise in a society with real social mobility is when different parties provide different levels of value. Where how much value you provide is directly related to the outcomes you receive. Since the outcomes you receive are directly equal to what you provided, inequality cannot exist. If 2 people provide the same amount of value, they will have the same outcomes.

For the first time in history, with unfuckable, private, PoW money, the social status of everyone and the individual way of life become truly flexible.

The ability to move upwards in the social hierarchy is cemented via economic incentive, because those at the bottom of the socio-economic ladder from all types of disadvantage can officially save and live by low time preference principles to build wealth, which allows for long term vision and strategic planning that is solely limited by an individuals or collectives ability.

Just as importantly, downward mobility also exists because those "at the top" are no longer able to socialize their losses due to their ability to control and exert influence over a population which has been a consequence of the control over money.

PoW brings back consequences to actions for everybody, not just the non-powerful.

The principles apply equally to everyone. If you are able to create value, do more work, provide a superior service/build a superior product or just generally make better choices in life, you will climb, it is a mathematical certainty.

Conversely, if you engage in poor economic behaviours i.e. If you consume more than you produce, if you are wasteful with your resources, if you make bad investment decisions, then guess what, you can't print any more money. You will fall down the social ladder.

That is exactly how it should be.

That is true equality of opportunity, which is exactly what equality is.

The Return on Violence

A PoW system truly changes the dynamic between violence and the ability to conduct it. Under the current monetary system, an endless amount of funding becomes available to wasteful and unprofitable activities. Namely, governments are able to fund endless violent wars with no economics incentives not to.

A PoW system brings back true consequences to making poor financial decisions, since what you consume is limited by what you produce and what you produce is limited by the value you provide.

Since war is by its nature a wasteful endeavour, natural limits are placed on one ability to conduct it.

Business & Free Markets

Fiat money, by its nature distorts the prices of good and therefore distorts markets as a whole.

The filtering of money into unsustainable government funded doctrines means that markets receive distorted price signals and thus Entrepreneurs, Inventors, Investors, Manufacturers & suppliers are unable to accurately assess what the market (the people) wants.

This in turn, creates vast unnecessary waste, and probably more consequently, a huge amount of mis-allocated capital (respective to providing value to society and humanity).

An example of this is the property market. When interest rates are artificially low, since the credit is created out of thin air, borrowers are incentivised to buy properties as it is easy, cheap money that they are not able to otherwise obtain. This in turn drives up prices and in turn incentivises others to purchase assets simply because they the price to go up.

In the case of property, sure, land becomes more valuable over time but the demand for the land has not increased exponentially, what has increased exponentially is the amount of quite literally, endless money available to real estate, which has been the driver of prices in the sector.

Compare this to a hard money credit market where the price of money (the interest rate) is set by a true free market of supply vs demand. Market participants are then forced to think and assess whether and approximate 5-10% interest rate is something that they are willing to pay vs the other potential investment benefits they could reap with their capital in other .

The answer is often that these associated costs force out many purely speculative market participants and force them to be more productive with their capital rather than participate in fake financialization growth.

For an example in regards to manufacturing and producing real world goods, Let's use the "I, Pencil" example for the amount of financial communication that occurs to bring a pencil together. Participants from all corners of the globe, speaking entirely different languages and all living in entirely different conditions, come together to play a part in producing the pencil, based purely on economic signals. From the rubber in the pencils, the wood, the compressed graphite but even extend that out to the producers of the machinery required to make the pencil and then extend that out to the miners of the minerals required to make the machinery that makes the machinery, extend that out to the manufacturers of that mining equipment, so on and so forth. Thousands if not hundreds of thousands of people communicate simply through economic signals to produce a pencil.

When market signals are distorted because the government funnels fiat to whatever agenda it sees fit on a localised time frame, or as another example, when fake money printed flows into Wall Street, Nasdaq or some VCs, what do you think entrepreneurs will do?

They will follow the money. It is only a natural reaction. Due to the size of capital that has been flowed into these areas, the distortion becomes further exacerbated.

Conversely to all of this, with true market signals on a hard money, consumers become the new price signal. In turn, producers get a real, organic signals of what the market (the people) needs and will then deliver solutions to those problems. Delivering true value to business, consumers, markets and humanity as a whole.

The Environment

The fiat monetary system fuels and incredible amount of wastage of our natural resources. The majority of which, is consumption wastefulness.

Think about the amount of resources wasted on the following, which is entirely fuelled by the ability to print money out of thin air. These can be via government spending or as a consequence of the Cantillon effect.

- Defence & Military
- Subsidising materials which kill the earth (cheap plastics/industries with toxic waste)
- Banks, Governments and other accessories to the financial system.
- Blind consumerism and excessive consumption driven by an increasing money supply.

This does not count the rest of the countries around the world and the copious amount of paper, cotton, plastics, fossil fuels and metals used to mint "money". The amount of resources needed to store cash and the amount of resources needed to move cash all around the world.

A tremendous waste of resources.

Which is why I find it funny when the fiat fuelled politicians and organisation attack PoW for not being "energy efficient" and also blame it for "melting the polar caps". It is an obvious cop out.

Junk

Plastics are yet another example of the fiat fuelled problems.

Why are they used? Because they're cheap

Why are they cheap? Plastic manufacturers are directly subsidised by their government, along with the Petro dollar system.

On a hard money standard, as opposed to easy money, people are not only more concerned about where they spend their hard-earned money due to the need for productive activities (which in itself, would likely solve much of the exponential waste problems) however also, because the government would no longer be able to support unproductive, unfeasible activities such as plastic manufacturing subsidies, the real cost of plastics and other disposable junk that pollutes the environment would be much higher. Thus, meaning that less plastics would be used and less junk would be created.

This aforementioned impact of reducing fiat does not even take into account the incredible waste of materials that have been ripped out of the earth to make the countless amounts of infrastructure that are not being used.

Health

Yes, believe it or not, fiat money directly harms the overall health of society when talking about probable choices made by consumers due to the underlying economic incentive structures.

These fake foods which I call "fiat foods" are the direct result of government subsidized, large scale industrial "food" manufacturing. Whether those subsidies come in the form of direct tax cuts, low interest rate loans (money fresh from the printer so to speak), direct tax cuts, regulatory shields or the increase of money flowing into the publicly listed companies. Fiat is mathematically fuelling the increase in availability of fake foods to consumers.

1) Previously unsustainable industries become sustainable

And 2) the devaluation of purchasing powers leads to the economic probability that some will buy "the cheaper, worse for you" foods such as seed oils, high carb foods and fake foods like chicken nuggets.

Traditionally, we have had to cultivate the land and sell those products in an open & free market, that is an equal playing field for all. A system that led to much better nutritional outcomes.

The artificial economic incentive structures fuelled by fiat, skew people towards high fat, high sugar, high calorie, high seed oil diets with little to no real nutritional value but a lower economic cost.

All of this due to fiat.

The cantillionaires who benefit most from this, only have the capacity to what they do based on their proximity to the state and its printing press. This however comes at the cost to everyone else.

Additionally, whilst pharmaceuticals can and have played a role in the longevity and quality of human life in many areas, there are still many pharmaceutical products that have been known to be prescribed to a level that causes damage in a society such as Percocet & Ritalin (meth) for kids and also pharmaceutical products that are largely ineffective.

For example, while sometimes useful, antidepressants are also often ineffective band aid solutions that don't solve the real reasons for why someone may be depressed, including the increased economic hardship created by the control over fiat. They instead just seek to change the receptors in the brain instead of actually trying to solve the root issue. Pain killers too, have been largely attributed to the rise in illicit opioid use, due to the monopolization of usage and lack of free market alternatives in many situations.

The point of talking about pharmaceuticals, is that the pharmaceutical industry has been able to produce these products and monopolize their use in an inefficient market, due to the loans available to them via artificially controlled interest rates, brought about by the central bank's monetary policy and also due to the increase in capital through stock valuation, brought about by a realignment of supply and demand.

If we want to take control of our health once again, we must take control of our money by opting out of the fiat Ponzi.

Politics & Government

Politics and government are fundamentally changed, as the politicians who make inefficient promises and promises that genuinely don't help the people are no longer able to print money out of thin air to support their agendas and thus are not able to buy the votes to get elected and are forced to be honest and tax people to fund an agenda.

This leads us towards a system where more honest and intelligent people are more likely to obtain power over a given period of time. Pretty much every politician you see today would be ousted over a long enough period of time due to these principles. Lies and deceit has unfortunately always been part and parcel of politics, however, moving back to a hard money standard skews the probabilities of inefficient operators not getting elected and at minimum, doesn't allow for the excessive buying and pork barrelling to non-productive means.

As we move into the next part of the chapter, I just want to highlight that all of these aforementioned problems just cement the reasoning for why only a money that requires PoW can be the solution to those searching for true prosperity and equality. A money that does not distort everything in the system as the current money distorts all the "yard sticks" of society.

What does privacy solve?

In addition to being PoW based, money must also be private, as so we can effectively fight the openly discussed technocratic agendas being advertised by many governments and organisations. Not only for the current challenges that we face but more importantly, to be the strongest money for all challenges and adversaries that may also arise in the future. Put Simply, to be a successful "unfuckable" money, it must be a PoW based, private money.

As mentioned earlier, the globalists and their technocracy are not going to go down easily without a fight. In fact, they are going to "throw the kitchen sink" at anyone trying to "rain on their parade".

They will still implement a social credit score and punish the behaviours of people participating in activities that are misaligned with their agenda's i.e., using cryptocurrencies or even buying meat for that matter.

In short, this is why Bitcoin, and most other "coins" are not a viable option. Because of KYC and transparency, it would still be very easy to implement a largely effective social credit system based on Bitcoin.

To those unfamiliar, tracing transactions does not involve a few people sitting down, "following the trail" and trying to keep all the numbers in their head or drawing lines between addresses on a whiteboard.

These tracing and tracking processes are already highly automated, with companies such as Chainalysis and CipherTrace already offering products to governments and corporations wishing to trace addresses.

These companies map a large amount of addresses to certain users/real world entities. They have numerous "products" that can automatically perform a whole range of activities such as tracing "financial crimes", making sure addresses comply with AML requirements. Importantly too, they are able to trace the origins of coins in an address and implement a risk score of the users based on the history of their coins.

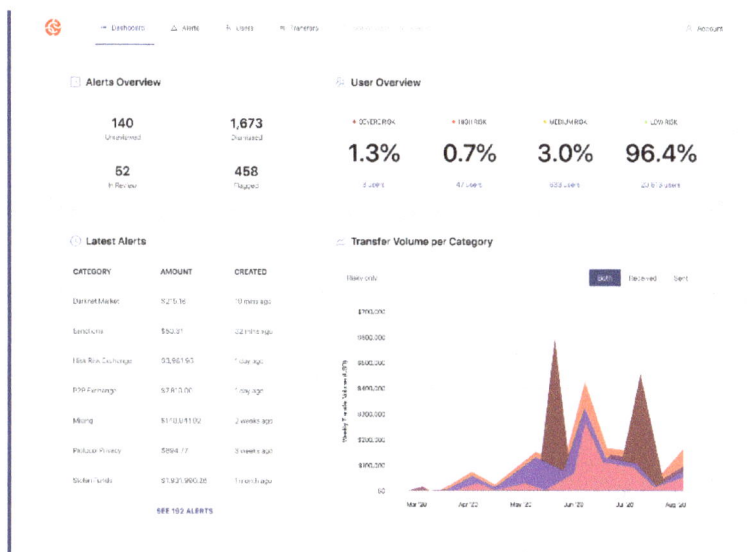

Here is an example of a wallet score.

This means due to the KYC of all addresses, from individuals to business, addresses and behaviours can be tied together and from which, a "risk score" can be devised. For example, if a consumer goes to a store and wants to make a purchase, that purchase can be tied to users to create a score. Additionally, if a user has "tainted" coins, this could lead to legal issues for the owner of the bitcoin, in a sense its like having a dollar bill that "still has all the cocaine that has ever touched it". This makes a traceable system like Bitcoin absolutely no different from CBDC's in the sense that you can implement a social credit score.

Trying to get around this with behaviours such as sending coins to non-KYC addresses i.e., a fresh wallet that is not tied to you, or sending coins to a mixer/coinjoining, will be seen as medium/high risk behaviour which will affect your social credit score accordingly. Similarly to how refusing to submit a roadside breath test for alcohol is seen the same as high range drink driving.

It is also important to note that because they can rate the origins of specific coins, it means that some coins will inherently be worth more than others. I.e., coins that have come from the black market, fraud, child porn etc, will naturally not be as desirable or have the same value as coins that have no history and even potentially come from "green" miners. This leaves us with a whole range of qualitative factors that would leave each coin with a certain value. This importantly means that all coins are not fungible. As we discussed earlier, fungibility is one of the characteristics of money, and without it, it cannot be effective money, let alone an effective digital cash.

Additionally, because all transactions are broadcast publicly to the miners in plain text, miners are able to decipher who is sending how much to who. Frighteningly, this means that because of the centralizing economic incentive structure of ASIC based mining, regulators can effectively implement blacklists upon major miners, so they don't process the transactions of addresses who have been participating in too many non-approved activities, making the coins akin to CBDC's.

To be clear, the economic incentive structure of ASIC miners means that a majority of the hashing power comes from large "factories". Run by companies who will all but oblige when the alternative is "getting their door kicked in", their 100's of millions of dollars of equipment getting seized and then being thrown in front of a judge.

The only solution to all of this is privacy.

Not only is privacy preferred by the normal person (i.e., you wouldn't want the whole world seeing your finances) but it also puts to bed any of the tools or technocratic systems that are being openly discussed.

Social credit scores would be impossible to implement on a private money as there is no data by which they can draw on to link addresses and rate the quality of purchases according to their schedule.

Additionally, since the transactions are sent to the miners with an encryption technique called ring signatures (we will get into this more next chapter), miners are unable to determine anything about the transaction other than if it is valid (i.e., the funds are in the wallet). This means that unlike transparent coins, it is not akin to a CBDC that can be censored nor have a social credit score implemented on it.

Why can't they kick down the door of miners of privacy coins?

The answer is simple, it is because the economic incentive structures behind mining Monero are different. Because of the hashing algorithm, the most efficient way of mining Monero is on a CPU, in other words, a normal computer. This means that mining is performed in a much more distributed manner, mining is performed by the everyday person who already has a computer and doesn't need to spend $10,000 for 1 specialized miner, nor will mining largely centralize in the areas/nations with cheap electricity. This is because the hashing algorithm "RandomX", designed by Howard Chu, makes it incredibly inefficient to mine with ASIC miners and thus economically impossible to do. We will get more into RandomX in the next chapter.

But can't we just change the system somehow and go back onto a gold standard? Where the money is "hard" i.e., requires PoW and is private?

The TL/DR is no.

Here's why...

Think of history as being made up from 2 factors:

1) An erratic/random component that consists of mostly unpredictable events that do not follow an inherently logical pattern, and
2) A predictable component that consists of long-term historical trends.

We're going to set 3 logical precedents to illustrate why.

Logical precedent 1:

"If a SMALL change is made that affects a long-term historical trend, then the effect of that change will almost always be transitory—the trend will soon revert to its original state.

(Example: A reform movement designed to clean up political corruption in a society rarely has more than a short-term effect; sooner or later the reformers relax and corruption creeps back in. The level of political corruption in a given society tends to remain constant, or to change only slowly with the evolution of the society. Normally, a political clean up will be permanent only if accompanied by widespread social changes; a SMALL change in the society won't be enough.)

The first principle is almost a tautology. If a trend were not stable with respect to small changes, it would wander at random rather than following a definite direction; in other words, it would not be a long-term trend at all."

This first precedent tells us that to change our current course of history. A radical change needs to be made. A change that would alter us away from the use of fiat money that props up increasingly dystopian regimes that we are experiencing. Small changes to the current system will not change anything.

Thus, a revolution of sorts would be required to change the trajectory. This does not necessarily mean an armed & violent uprising but rather a revolution that can be achieved by not playing with the cards we are dealt with in society… the cards that would favour those who implement the system at play for their own gain. In other words, shifting to a new monetary system that can't be manipulated unlike fiat.

Logical Precedent 2:

"If a change is made that is sufficiently large to alter permanently a long-term historical trend, then it will alter the society as a whole. In other words, a society is a system in which all parts are interrelated, and you can't permanently change any important part without changing all other parts as well."

This importantly shows us that establishing a new system will alter society as we see it. It won't just simply affect what money we use, but rather show us that the entire way of life will be shifted away from a dystopian digital panopticon to a lasting change in society that alters the societal incentive structures and ultimately changes the outcomes in many parts of society.

Logical precedent 3:

"These principles result from the complexity of human societies. A change in human behaviour will affect the economy of a society and its physical environment; the economy will affect the environment and vice versa, and the changes in the economy and the environment will affect human behaviour in complex, unpredictable ways; and so forth.

The network of causes and effects is far too complex to be untangled and understood.

People do not consciously and rationally choose the form of their society. Societies develop through processes of social evolution that are not under rational human control."

These aforementioned precedents are not laws of physics but rather just logical thoughts or guides to historical precedents, if you will.

The precedents mentioned also illustrate why it is hopelessly difficult to reform the current monetary system in such a way that would lead it onto another course that prevents it from progressively narrowing our sphere of freedom and enhancing the power of the few who benefit from the control of the fiat monetary system.

As outlined in chapter 4, we can see that technology at large has been applied to strengthen "the system", at what has generally been a high expense to individual liberty and sovereignty. The technologies that have been implemented in society today and the cultural attitudes, do not contrast that view.

Changes large enough to make a lasting difference in favour of freedom could not be initiated from within because it would be realized that they would disrupt the system far too much that anyone who makes the rules and benefits from them, could never accept the new modus operandi.

So, any attempts at reform could only ever be too toothless to be effective. Even if changes large enough to make a lasting difference were initiated, they would be retracted when their disruptive effects became apparent.

Thus, permanent changes in favour of freedom can only be brought about only by persons prepared to accept radical change of the entire monetary system that props up the current global power structure.

In other words, by revolutionaries, not reformers. And in other words, by the ordinary people, not by those in charge.

Centralized technology and freedom are not compatible.

Now we have established that 2 principles are required to solve the problems the world faces, and that "revolution" is required. we should start looking at something that is:

1) PoW limited.
2) Provides private transactions.
3) A technology that is outside of the current system.

That is Monero.

It is through these principles that Monero truly becomes what Bitcoin maxi's dream Bitcoin could be.

It is truly a protocol that is permissionless, where no central authority can come and determine arbitrarily what is and isn't to be.

It is a monetary network that is truly open for long lasting prosperity, that doesn't discriminate nor has any gatekeepers, unlike the fiat monetary system.

It is a protocol that cryptographically solves all the problems you have when you spend fiat or bitcoin. It is truly private and It is truly censorship resistant.

Chapter 6

The Monero Bible

Now that we have determined that to fix many problems in the world and to provide a platform for equal prosperity and freedom, we must have something that is:

1) Private
2) Uses PoW
3) Revolutionary

This is where I am introducing Monero. A Private, PoW based, revolutionary technology.

That's why I have broken it down in a way that is very understandable by normal people. I very much dislike the complexity of a lot of Monero documents and explainers that I have seen around, quite simply some of them are ridiculously & frustratingly complicated for the average non-tech idiot like myself.

What will separate those who are going to make it from the rest is their propensity to actually understand the major concepts and see how they are applicable as a solution to the problems previously discussed in earlier chapters (not the actual maths and cryptography itself, so don't worry too much if it doesn't make sense at first… especially if you don't have a background in the field of maths, crypto, blockchain, cryptography etc)

It is important to understand the real stuff behind what makes Monero the way it is, through understanding comes confidence and trust.

The mathematicians and developers responsible for designing and keeping Monero safe are let's be honest, a bit unhinged when it comes to their understanding of the incredibly complicated cryptography and coding that is Monero. What they understand is just simply not understandable by 99.9% of the population.

With that said, to go on a 100 page rant about the Monero technical design would actually probably be a bit antithetical to the purpose of this book.

For those interested, the best resource (that I found) for Monero giga brain mathematical and cryptographic concepts is "Zero-to-Monero: a technical guide to a private digital currency; for beginners, amateurs, and experts" by koe , Kurt M. Alonso and Sarang Noether… shout out to those guys. As well as Mastering Monero by Serhack.

Be warned though, it is not for everybody.

If you think this is hard to follow (which I hope you don't). Boy oh boy, you're in for a shock when you read Zero to Monero or Mastering Monero. I would even be lying if I said I understood on any meaningful level, the PHD level cryptography and maths.

I want to build up your knowledge base surrounding Monero and the best place to start is with the history of Monero, the fundamentals of Monero and the Monero technical design.

Let's go.

Starting with the **History of Monero.**

If you are really into Monero or have been in Monero for some time, a lot of this at the beginning will be second nature, however you will more than likely still get a lot from this chapter.

The history of Monero really began in 2008, when Satoshi published the whitepaper for Bitcoin. The whitepaper was titled *"Bitcoin: A Peer-to-Peer Electronic Cash System".* Key words here, Bitcoin was designed to be a peer-to-peer digital cash.

We have touched on the characteristics of money and currency earlier in the book. Bitcoin clearly does not meet the definition of cash as it is not fungible, a problem that affects Bitcoin to this day. 1 Bitcoin ≠ 1 Bitcoin in many circumstances.

It is because of these issues and Satoshi's original goal of *"A Peer-to-Peer Electronic Cash System"* that Monero was created.

Monero was created to be everything that Bitcoin aspired to be. A peer-to-peer digital cash.

First however, the base infrastructure needed to be created. It was the creation of the CryptoNote protocol in 2012 by an anonymous person or group of people known as Nicholas Van Saberhagen, that allowed the base infrastructure for Monero to exist.

Bytecoin was the first coin launched on the CryptoNote protocol. Without going into an exhaustive history about Bytecoin. It was and still is generally considered by those around at the time that Bytecoin had a "scammy" vibe to it. Bytecoin had an 80% stealth pre-mine which means that 80% of the total supply was given to the developers in order to enrich themselves but they hid it from everyone else. On top of this, there had been a story made up to say that Bytecoin had actually been around for a few years to justify the reason there was so many coins in existence, where in fact it was due to the premine. Many people were able to see through this very quickly.

The general community sought to hard fork Bytecoin however with a "fair launch". As the underlying privacy technology was promising.

Fun fact: Monero means "coin" in Esperanto.

The first fork called BitMonero was first launched on the 17th of April 2014. Importantly, BitMonero was a codebase fork of Bytecoin, not a hard fork from byte coin. Which means that while it used the same code base, it did not inherit the history, the pre-mine or the general "scammyness" of Bytecoin.

The BitMonero Fork away from Bytecoin was launched by a guy who goes by the name of "Thankful_for_today" who initially forked it, made binaries available and then stuck around to provide support to the general community.

The BitMonero fork wasn't initially received well by the broader crypto community.

According to Riccardo Spagni aka "fluffypony" who explained on a podcast, that 10 days after launch, a small group of contributors including himself had been having disagreements about the general direction of the protocol.

Following which, the 2 "factions" decided to separate paths and from which a majority of the community had followed the latter group who did not include "thankful_for_today".

Fun fact: 10 days after launch Monero had approximately 7400 h/s (hashes per second)

Fun Fact: The first OTC trade for Monero was 1000 XMR for 0.5 BTC. BTC was at around $500.

As a result, the community had essentially begun to improve upon itself. The name of the project was changed from "BitMonero" to "Monero", which as I mentioned earlier, means "coin" in Esperanto.

The first team of Monero had 5 developers, 3 of them were anonymous, 2 were publicly known. Probably the most well-known one today is Riccardo Spagni aka "fluffypony" followed closely by Francisco Cabañas aka "ArticMine".

Because Monero was launched on the CryptoNote protocol, all of the infrastructure needed to be rebuilt vs having a fork of Bitcoin, where the infrastructure was largely existent. Remember, this is the early days of crypto where crypto was exponentially less developed than it is today.

It was from these beginnings that Monero was created. Now, privacy and PoW in Money was to become a reality for anyone who wanted it. A revolutionary invention that was not fully appreciated at the time and probably still isn't appreciated adequately today.

Without writing an entire chapter on the early history of Monero, that fairly well sums up all we need to know about the very early history to understand how Monero will play a role in a strong world.

Important subtle notes to take that haven't been mentioned and are not overtly obvious to the untrained eye, are that Monero had absolutely no Pre-Mine of token and in addition, doesn't use Proof-Of-Stake (POS) as a consensus or governance mechanism.

Along the way, Monero has made many improvements to the protocol to increase privacy to the users of the protocol. For example, the implementation of Bulletproofs to reduce transaction sizes. If you want a full list of all the improvements, go to the roadmap on getmonero.org.

Moving forward into the next interesting and I feel significant phase of Monero's journey. Because of Monero's ability to perform anonymous and private transaction, it has begun to be widely accepted on the dark net... Naturally, this in fact is a very important moment in Monero's history, and indeed repetitious of the history of nearly all successful technologies.

As when a technology is adopted by criminals, it does not prove that it is a bad technology, it simply proves that the technology works and also provides an advantage the those who adopt it. Take phones as an example, criminals were the first to adopt phones as it allowed them to organise their business with completely new potential, unsurveilled (at the time) by law enforcement. Cars too were adopted first by bank robbers as it allowed them to escape the scene of the crime at a rate faster than any Law enforcement could keep up.

The fact that these technologies were adopted and used by criminals was not and is not a reason to ban them or attack the technology, it is just proof that the new technology works as intended, there are many multipurpose benefits and as such, completely new ways of life and society can exist.

In this regard, Monero is not different from previous technological innovations. The fact that it was AND STILL IS used on the Dark Net, goes to show that it is indeed a truly strong and resilient technology.

A technology that provides value to whoever decides to use it, even under the most adversarial circumstances possible.

That dark net proves that Monero gives monetary freedom under all circumstances. A concept that has been lost to the modern world and certainly has never been seen in a globalised, digital world.

Now we have covered the history, let's move into the technical factors and the technical design.

This book is written for the layman to understand so it would be antithetical to talk PHD level and lose 90% of readers. Distribution and understanding of conceptual information, is what will give any new technology the best chance of success.

Without any further ado, happy learning.

Proof of work

Proof of work is the mining method in which miners commit their hashing power (real world resource) to facilitate and process transactions on the network.

The concept was invented in 1993 to as a system to prevent email spam, however it never took off at the time.

The significance of Proof-of-Work is that it brings consequences back to malicious actions. If someone wants to attack the network, it expends real world resources that have a cost to them thus limiting the potential for malicious behaviour. "Attacking the network" could be something as simple as submitting false transactions or something as serious as a 51% attack.

The purpose of proof-of-work algorithms is proving that certain work was carried out, that a computational puzzle was "solved" and also deterring manipulation of data by establishing large energy and hardware-control requirements to be able to do so i.e. securing the network from a 51% attack.

Monero uses RandomX hashing algorithm to create hashes.

RandomX hashing algorithm + CPU Mining

Don't worry about the initial confusing Ness of the words hashing algorithm.

Put simply, through a hashing algorithm, transactions and blocks on the Monero network can be mathematically verified to be authentic or illegitimate. Thus, be approved or declined so to say.

RandomX is a proof-of-work (PoW) algorithm (Remember, Monero is a proof-of-work based coin) that is optimized for use on general-purpose CPUs i.e., the everyday persons computer.

RandomX uses something called random code execution (hence the name, RandomX) together with several "memory-hard techniques" (don't worry about this) to disincentivise the ability of specialised mining hardware such as ASIC miners to join the network and ultimately dominate the hashing power, which would lead to the increased centralisation of the mining process such as we see on Bitcoin.

The significance of RandomX is that now, the hashing power is economically disincentivized away from centralized providers such as we see with "ASIC mining farms" on the bitcoin network and pushed back into the hands of everyday people. Making the network far more decentralized (which if you remember, is the point of cryptocurrency)

Not only does this avoid the inevitability that mining becomes centralised in the hands a few but it also means that the everyday person no matter how big or how small can use their existing hardware i.e. their laptop to mine unlike Bitcoin where laptop mining is beyond dead as you need spend what is an unachievable or impractical amount for most, on expensive specialized equipment.

Additionally, the requirement for specialized equipment required on Bitcoin also ads an extra layer of trust required in the ecosystem, because as Richard heart (yes, I know, he's a scammer) correctly says, "you have to suck middleman d*ck to get a Bitcoin miner"… with that middle man being BitMain (the producer of most Bitcoin miners) or one of the select other ASIC providers which you also have to provide KYC to obtain a miner.

To reinforce, the main advantage of RandomX is that it democratises and decentralizes the mining process far beyond anything Bitcoin and ASIC based coins could dream of. Not only is PoW far more decentralized than PoS, but CPU based PoW is far more decentralized than ASIC based PoW, making it the ultimate form of PoW.

Ring signatures

Essentially, they are the cryptographic method they use to "sign transactions", meaning that it is the way they prove that the transaction is valid and comes from the legitimate user/owner of the funds.

BUT, importantly, this method of signing keeps the identity of the sender completely anonymous/obfuscated unlike Bitcoin and nearly every other coin.

Essentially, A ring signature makes use of your "account key" (which is your address etc) and then presents it alongside a number of other publicly known "keys" pulled randomly from other Blockchain transactions.

Ultimately meaning that an outside observer can't tell who the transaction belongs to, because in a "ring" of possible signers, all ring members are probabilistically equal.

Ring signatures ensure that transactions are untraceable to specific users. This by consequence, ensures that there are no fungibility issues with Monero, since specific coins can't be linked to previous users or activities. So even if an adversary knows your key signature (which is nearly, if not completely impossible to find out given the proper care) you are still mixed up in a "ring" of other signers.

This method of obfuscation is why chain surveillance firms such as Chainalysis and CipherTrace cannot trace any transaction to and from any specific address/people.

Currently the ring size is 16, meaning there is you + 15 other signers = 16 Signatures. With plans to increase the number of signatures in a ring in the future.

Ring CT

RingCT is short for Ring Confidential Transactions.

This method of cryptography is how transaction amounts (output amounts) on Monero transactions are hidden from outside observers. Naturally, only the sender and receiver know the amount spent/received although the receiver will not know who it is from, the sender will know which address they sent it to otherwise how would they send it to them in the first place.

Ring Confidential transactions were adopted in January 2017 at block height #1220516.

After September 2017, this feature became mandatory for all transactions on the network in order to avoid holes in security and privacy and to make it easier for users to gain the full amount of privacy available.

RingCT introduced an improved version of ring signatures called "A Multi-layered Linkable Spontaneous Anonymous Group signature".. yes, I know, a cryptographers dream and a normal person nightmare. To cut through the annoyingly difficult jargon, this allows for amounts, origins and destinations involved transactions to be kept hidden, that's at least the best way to keep it simple.

Stealth address' aka One-time address

A Stealth Address aka one time address is an automatically created one-time public address (otherwise known as a random, one-time address) that is created by the sender, on behalf of the recipient, when a transaction on the Monero network is initiated.

Since, this is all automatically done on the backend, there is no need to worry about it being too difficult...essentially you can't mess it up.

Pedersen commitments/Range Proofs

Pedersen commitments are a cryptographic method that allow a prover to commit a value without revealing it or being able to change it.

In simple language, this means that the amount of coins sent by the sender and received by the receiver are the same. If you are not in crypto, this may not have too much meaning, however, this is important in proving that coins can not be created out of thin air in a process called "double spending".

This in essence allows the supply of Monero to be verified. Since the block reward (Coinbase transaction) is public and Pedersen commitments make it impossible to double spend, you can accurately arrive at the supply of Monero in existence.

Dynamic Block Size

For those In crypto, ask yourself, how many times have you seen a project or just something in general life where it seems like its absolute gold per se, an absolute gem and you can't believe everyone isn't using it or if its new, you think every single person should be using it, but when it comes down to it, it's just too hard to use by most people or has another issue that ultimately just means it can never scale to 8 billion people?

Probably a few times, I can think of a few examples.

Ultimately, what decides whether something will be successful is its ability to scale not only after its launch but to a level of mainstream adoption where every man and his dog can use it.

Dynamic block size is the not so secret weapon that Monero employs to allow for ultra-level scaling, no matter how big or small it may be at the time.

I found an article that best explains the importance dynamic block sizes and while I can paraphrase it, would rather keep the snippet in its original beauty.

"Bitcoin has a block size limit, which means once enough transactions are included in a block, any additional transactions will have to wait in line for the next block. A helpful analogy would be thinking about a train. A train pulls up to the station, and those in line file in. Once the train is full, anyone left outside will have to wait for the next one.

Bitcoin uses fees to determine who gets into the block or not. Jumping back to the train analogy, one can imagine one potential passenger, that is about to be left behind, offers the train engineer five dollars to give him a seat. Other passengers follow suit, and eventually there is a bidding war to see who gets which seats. It's up to the driver to decide if he wants to honour the first come, first serve policy, but it's in his best financial interest to maximize his income by taking the highest bidders on board.

In this analogy, miners are the train drivers. They can include whatever transactions they want in the block, but they will generally choose the ones that have the highest paid fees.

Alternatively, if blocks are not very full, people have no incentive to pay high fees because there are plenty of free seats to spare.

In the height of the 2017 cryptocurrency boom, Bitcoin was flooded with transactions, and the fees skyrocketed for those that wanted to be included in the next block, or any near-future block for that matter.

Those who were unwilling to pay high fees saw their transactions pushed back for hours, days, or even drop out of the queue altogether.

This was a harrowing insight into how Bitcoin would fare if the oft talked about 'mass adoption' were to occur. If Bitcoin was to be used by the masses, things would be even worse than in 2017, and Bitcoin would be inaccessible to anyone but the wealthy, simply because the throughput is small due to a fixed block size, causing the fee market to take over.

Monero foresaw this and wanted to do something different. So, the Monero developers implemented a dynamic block size.

Basically, Monero also has a block size cap, but it's a soft cap. When the line of waiting transactions gets too long, the miners can increase the size of the blocks. With our train analogy, you can imagine adding more train cars to fit the extra passengers. After the queue is empty the blocks shrink back to their original size going forward.

If this seems like a neat idea, it seems reasonable to ask why Monero is the only cryptocurrency that has implemented this. Why not add it on Bitcoin so as to put a stop to the throughput issues?

Unfortunately, this is not possible. There are several reasons why, and we'll do our best to explain.

It's always in a miner's best interest to have large blocks. With large blocks they can fit in more transactions, and make more money off of the fees, as well as the block rewards. This has the potential to lead to spam attacks, where someone sends many small transactions, with small fees, to bloat the chain. Miners would just raise the block size include them all because money is money, no matter how small. This would lead to consistently large blocks with little economic benefit. Bitcoin solves this by artificially restricting the block size, thereby generating a fee market. Spam attackers would have to out pay the other users in fees, and it is no longer cheap. But this means blocks get full leaving some transactions waiting as mentioned above.

So how can Monero have dynamic block sizes but avoid spam attacks? The answer is simple, but clever. A penalty on the block reward is introduced when a block is bigger than normal. If a miner wants to increase the block size, the reward they get from finding that block will be less than they would otherwise receive. So, they will only increase the block size when the paid transaction fees of the users outweigh the lost portion of the block reward. For example, if the miner would lose 0.5 XMR by raising the block reward, and the sum of the paid transaction fees would be 0.4 XMR, then there would be a net loss of 0.1 XMR if they were to raise the size, so they wouldn't do it. Conversely, if the total transaction fees added up to 0.7 XMR, then there would be a net gain of 0.2 XMR, even though they lose the 0.5 XMR from the block reward penalty, so the miner will increase the size.

These dynamic blocks, allow the network to grow organically, without artificially restricting the block size to make a forced fee market, while still avoiding spam attacks. There are several more angles we can view this idea from, and more reasons why it wouldn't be possible to add to Bitcoin, but for now, we hope that the reader has an understanding of how Monero sidesteps several of the problems in Bitcoin and its derivatives, and how it plans to scale its throughput into the future."

(Salazar, 2020)

I feel this sums up the concept and the importance of Dynamic block sizes perfectly in layman's terms.

Dynamic block sizes are the best way to scale a cryptocurrency-based monetary network, it allows flexibility for everyone to use it whilst also not damaging the decentralization of the network.

Moving on…

View Key Auditing

Monero has the ability to be partially optionally transparent. This is done through providing view keys to external parties such as accountants, financial advisors, regulators etc. Anyone who you wish to share your incoming finances with. Monero is not private with absolutely no option to be functionally transparent. By sharing a view key, a person is allowing access to view every incoming transaction for that address.

ED25519 Elliptic Curve

This is a subsection that could become incredibly complicated and boring, incredibly quickly if I wanted it to be. However, in short, this is Monero's elliptic curve, which in short means it's how Monero addresses are given to a user, in short, it's what protects users funds from others. It's what protects your wallet from being "hacked".

An elliptic curve works by choosing a random value along the curve and using that value to create the seed words.

How it does that is totally antithetical to the purpose of the book since it is incredibly detailed, mathematical and nuanced, so it's best to keep it simple for now.

An important thing to note is that it is different from Bitcoin's elliptic curve. This means that if in the future bitcoins elliptic curve is "cracked", it will not effect Monero.

P2Pool (and its resistance against 51%/attacks)

P2pool mining is actually a pretty niche concept.

As those in the space know, Mining pools are often used because whilst it doesn't increase your probability of solving a block or increase your hash power, it does mean that as a collective of people "pooling" or banding their hash power together, their collective probability of solving the block increases meaning that block/mining rewards can at least be more predictably obtained rather than getting a lump sum of block rewards all at once and then having to wait what is probably an average of 2-5 years to solve another block.

When I last did the maths approx. 12 months ago, it took an average of 4 years for 1 person with 1 miner (1000 h/s) to mine a block.

Sure, you might get lucky and get one on your first day or a few months in but as probability suggest, the longer you play the game, the closer to the median/average you get.

Unfortunately, traditional mining pools rely entirely on trust and ultimately can allow the pool owner/controller to act maliciously against the network with the hash power provided by the miners. For example, the pool operator could use your computational power to attack the network, attempt to double-spend funds (if the pool is large enough), or simply use the work being done by the miners to pay themselves and never reward miners properly for their work.

The biggest risk to a network is that of a pool (or multiple pools working together) having greater than 51% of the networks hash rate under their control, as they could use this to cheat and spend funds twice (a double-spend attack) or attempt to change the rules of the network.

It's unlikely but it is still possible, and that is the important thing to consider (to those not in crypto reading this book, I have noticed that normies tend to trust a lot more than people within the crypto space, they tend to want to see the good in everyone and believe me, I see the good in everyone, but I don't trust everyone to be in control of my freedom, which is what control of the monetary system is. As the saying in crypto goes... Don't trust, verify). It's not so much the operators of the pools but rather if someone were to compromise those pools like a state actor, serious damage could be done... at least in the short term... unnecessary damage that could be avoided by being a little smarter i.e., by having a technology like P2Pool.

The solution to this dilemma is P2Pool (a play on the concept of Peer to peer and mining pools).

P2Pool was originally created for mining Bitcoin back in 2011. Unfortunately for the Bitcoin network, it never achieved the widespread adoption that it deserves and to this day remains largely unused. Not gonna lie, I have no idea why.

Thankfully, one of the key developers behind RandomX, SChernykh, spent his vacation coming up with solutions to some of the issues with the Bitcoin implementation of P2Pool and re-writing all of the software from scratch.

P2Pool in Monero allows for a completely trust-less way for miners to work together to solve blocks and secure the Monero network by using special node software for P2Pool in order to share the work.

This is done using a new blockchain (a "sidechain") that keeps a record of the work each miner performs, their wallet address, and how much Monero they have earned, and then pays the reward out in a trust-less and decentralized way. As this sidechain has far fewer miners, it's much easier to find and submit blocks on it than on the main Monero network, making it easier for miners to get consistent pay outs versus mining Monero alone.

So, how does P2Pool actually solve the drawbacks of pool mining?

In P2Pool, there is no centralized pool, centralized pool operator, or single person holding onto funds and distributing payouts. All the work being collectively done by those mining via P2Pool is checked by the P2Pool blockchain and other node operators to ensure that it is legitimate, and all miners are paid out according to the work they have done immediately when a block is found directly from the rewards in that found block.

When miners choose to use P2Pool instead of a centralized pool, they remove all power and trust from pool operators and ensure that their work contributes to the good of the network and to their own rewards, reduce the risk of network attacks, misuse of their work, or theft of rewards that they are owed.

Not only does this help them protect their own interests, it also reduces the risk that centralized pools can pose to the Monero network as a whole. P2Pool usage also helps immensely to reduce the risk that nation-states or regulators could pose to the health of the network, as there are no centralized pool operators to pressure, no geographical concentration of pools to lean on, or any other easy point of pressure for them to use against Monero.

Chapter 7

Monero vs Bitcoin

I think Monero vs Fiat or any other shitcoin would not be a relevant comparison. It would be like putting 19 year old Mike Tyson in the ring with a 12 year old skinny white boy (me when I was 12).

Truth be told, that was actually the message that I was trying to get across. Not because I hate fiat but because maths doesn't lie.

Just in case I haven't been clear, fiat money is a Ponzi and is designed to empower the rich and provide an overarching infrastructure for control of what in one form or another, surmounts to the entire globe.

Proof of Stake Shitcoins are a replication of the fiat system by creating money out of thin air and distributing it as they see fit.

Whilst putting to bed the bugaboo of fiat myths, we must now focus on Bitcoin who is by Market Cap the largest cryptocurrency, for good reason.

The very fact that I am using Bitcoin as the "competitor" to Monero, and not one of the thousands of shitcoins that claims to be money, goes to show that I do indeed think highly of Bitcoin and the community, despite minor differences.

It is like debating an intelligent person vs debating an idiot. Sure, you would debate an intelligent person, but you would have to be an idiot to debate an idiot without tangible benefit. That is why I chose Bitcoin, because it is or at minimum was a powerful tool.

Full disclosure: I hold Bitcoin, will almost certainly continue to hold Bitcoin and also believe strongly in the mission of Bitcoin, I want it to work. I just see areas of weakness in a game theoretical sense which mean that over a long period of time, it has a lot of weakness's which are currently and likely to continue to be exploited or manipulated. We mentioned those weaknesses in previous chapters. In any case, I think Monero is without a doubt a much stronger tool regardless of whether those weaknesses lead to its demise or not. Subsequently, I think that Monero is the strongest tool that humanity has ever seen.

In my opinion, bitcoin is actually a very important cultural revolution. I however believe that Monero is the technological revolution that was intended to facilitate the cultural revolution. Both Cultural and techological revolutions are incredibly important in changing the current fiat system and power structures held up because of it.

Unlike many toxic Bitcoin maximalists, I think we are on the same team, in the same battle, fighting the same enemy.

The only difference is that we are fighting with different weapons. An axe vs a sword for example. Whether a sword or an axe is better is dependant on what you are trying to achieve.

Here in the chapter, we will go directly for the heart of Dracula and build on why privacy on the base layer is the only way to have a truly functioning and freedom enabling money.

First, we will look at a comparison between Monero, Bitcoin and other "money like" assets where possible. Then we will get into debunking the FUD bought forth by Bitcoiners and just general areas of concern that has been mentioned previously .

In chapter 1, we broke down the characteristics of money. Let's break down these characteristics of money between Bitcoin and Monero a bit further, to see which serves as a better money.

Characteristics of money

	Monero	Bitcoin	Fiat	Gold
Limited supply	Soft cap	Hard cap @ 21,000,000	No cap	Soft cap
Fungible	Yes	No	Yes	Mostly Different values for bullion, ingot, coins etc
Portable	Yes	Yes	Yes	No
Dividable	Yes, 12 decimal places.	Yes, 8 decimal places.	Yes, 2 decimal places. i.e., 100 cents = 1 dollars	Yes but difficult
Durable	Yes	Yes	More or less	Yes
Acceptability	Dark Markets & growing outside	More than Monero but less than fiat. Still growing	Widely accepted... for now	Not really

Limited supply

Bitcoin has a limited supply of 21,000,000 BTC whilst on the other hand, Monero has an infinite maximum supply however it is limited at any given point in time. It cannot be artificially created, it can only be mined according to the emission schedule... exactly like Bitcoin except Bitcoin max's out at 21,000,000 BTC.

On the surface, it may appear to be a win for Bitcoin, and I would personally agree that a limited supply is better than an infinite supply if it is realistically possible to do so. In the same way I'd prefer everyone to be rich if it was possible, however it is not and cannot be possible.

In reality, it is not ideal to have a finite supply when talking about a decentralized cryptocurrency over the long term.

The Bitcoin block rewards are due to end in the year 2140. After that, no more Bitcoin will be mined and all 21,000,000 will be in circulation.

This, mathematically leads to some HUGE problems when it comes to transaction fees, as those who submit transactions to the layer 1 chains will be making up 100% of miner revenue, instead of the block reward subsidising the cost of transactions as it currently does.

Without a block reward or equivalent made up in transactions, the ability to afford the costs associated with securing the network (i.e., new miners, electricity bills et) is almost nil.

Additionally, the cost of base layer settlement will reach prices that are only affordable by a select few, meaning that only those who can justify the thousands of dollars in transaction fees (i.e., multimillion dollar settlements) can actually use Bitcoin in a capacity where they indisputably hold their own keys.

This means that miners and hash power will diminish, leaving the network vulnerable to attack. Whilst simultaneously making it very unaffordable for the everyday person to transact and settle transactions on the base chain.

Remember too, the problem with fiat is not that it inflates, as gold technically inflates as we see 1-2% per year. The real problem with fiat is its arbitrary inflation that is concocted by a select few, that also effects the entire population.

Monero's supply schedule is cryptographically mapped out, cannot change and is far lower than that of gold meaning that, as you see below, inflation asymptomatically approaches 0%, whilst still providing the incentive for miners to secure the chain forever.

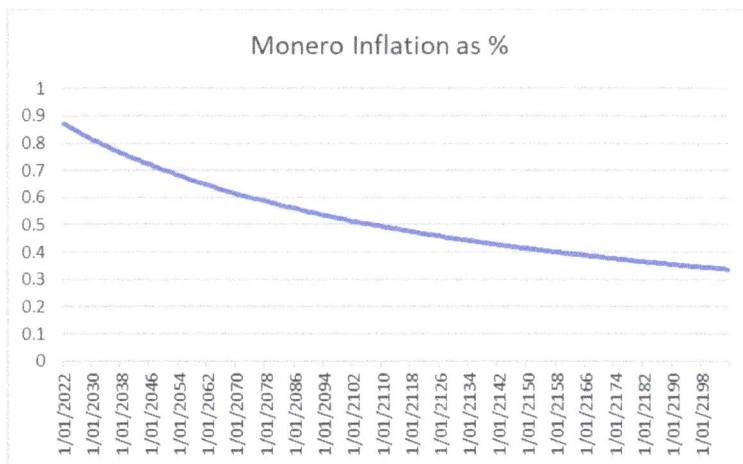

Monero Inflation as %

Monero is limited in supply at any given period of time because you know ahead of time what they supply will be. The supply cannot be more than what is cryptographically mapped out.

In my view, this is a clear win for Monero. As instead of focusing solely on a perceived benefit through a single number, the supply is instead used to design a workable system for the long term freedom and prosperity of humanity.

Fungibility

One of, if not the most important aspect of money when talking about its use as medium of exchange is fungibility.

Which to refresh, is where 1=1. Essentially where all the units are identical and indistinguishable thus meaning they have identical values.

A simple concept that it isn't always as easy to achieve as it seems.

Monero is fungible, because of the ability to hide the history (distinguishability) of any given coin (like cash). Therefore, all Monero inherently has the same desirability. 1=1. Any given coin is just as equal as the next one. Monero has no history and thus, the coins are indistinguishable. Completely uniform in the true sense of the word.

Contrary to the belief of some, Bitcoins themselves are 100% traceable back to the moment on inception and are not private or anonymous. This may not seem like a problem at first glance, however as this severely affects the desirability of each different coin.

Many coins are already considered tainted given the fact that they have participated in numerous activities such as online gambling, DarkNet markets, child porn websites or even something simple as the fact it may have come from a "green" miner vs say a north Korean miner… a whole range of activities could deem those coins a potential risk to their holder, meaning that each coin will have a different level of desirability based on its passed. This means that 1 does not equal 1. This means that Bitcoin is not fungible, it is not uniform, all the coins are distinguishable. The coins are not uniform.

This means that it is factually correct to say that Monero is fungible, and Bitcoin is not.

It is factually correct to say that something cannot be effectively as a money (Store of value and medium of exchange) if it is not fungible.

Fungibility is a hurdle requisite.

Portability

Both Monero and Bitcoin are equally portable. Both can be stored and spent from both "hot" and "cold" wallets.

Divisibility

Bitcoin is dividable into 8 decimal places, meaning that there are 100,000,000 (100 million) units called Satoshi's within a Bitcoin.

Monero is dividable into 12 decimal places, meaning that there are 100,000,000,000 (100 billion) units called Piconero's with a Monero.

The concept is exactly the same for Dollars and Cents.

In my opinion, I don't see a huge problem with the smaller number of decimal places in Bitcoin.

Both are acceptably divisible. However, if we are going to pick what is more divisible, then Monero is 1000x more divisible.

Durability

Similarly, the durability of both assets is practically the same.

The only thing I would mention in regard to durability, is that because certain UTXO sets can be blacklisted due to its lack of fungibility, it means that those Satoshi's/ Bitcoins are not durable in that sense. Likewise, the traceability of Bitcoin means that globalists and law enforcement can be led straight to the source of the Bitcoin i.e., the owner & in most cases, the seed phrase too.

There are arguments in regard to methods of storing the seed phrase in an underground bunker in the middle of the woods, engraved on a gold or silver plate that can negate that risk however many of the methods/knowledge is impractical when talking about adoption by 8 billion people.

However, the Bitcoin is still durable as the Bitcoin is not destroyed but simply not in the hands of the owner.

Acceptability

Bitcoin is currently more accepted by various good and service providers than Monero.

Monero is accepted on the DarkNet almost exclusively and is gaining traction into other good and service providers. Through the use of bridges and wallet features.

As mentioned already, the information in this book is designed to be as timeless as possible so I will not name any specific providers or services they offer. However, you can purchase nearly anything using Monero as a base currency.

Final Scorecard

	Monero	Bitcoin
Limited Supply	Y	Y
Fungibility	Y	
Portability	Y	Y
Durability	Y	Y
Divisibility	Y	Y
Acceptability	Y	Y

Quality of money score card:

Monero: 6

Bitcoin: 5

Cash: 5

Gold: 3

	MONERO	BITCOIN	FIAT MONEY
MAX SUPPLY	Infinite, however supply is cryptographically mapped	21,000,000 BTC	Infinite – Arbitrary expansion
CURRENT SUPPLY (at time of writting)	18,105,666	18,925,000	21,809,700,000,000,000
CONSENSUS MECHINISM	Proof Of Work	Proof Of Work	Washington/The Fed
BLOCK TIME	2 Minutes	10 Minutes	Whenever they feel like it
BLOCK SIZE	Dynamic block size	1MB	Brrrrrrrrr
BLOCK REWARD	0.60 XMR	6.25 BTC	Whatever they feel like
PRIVATE	100%	Nill, completely transparent	Clear as mud
HASHING ALGORITHM	RandomX	SHA-256	Brrrrrrrrrr
MINING EQUIPMENT	CPU Dominant	ASIC Dominant	The Brrrrr 5000

Features

	Monero	Bitcoin
Known/predictable supply	Yes	Yes
Cost to run a node	Runs on existing CPU's	$50
Ease of setting up a node	Very simple, GUI wallet, CLI wallet	Not easy. Minimum 10-20 Hours research
ASIC resistant	Yes, uses RandomX algorithm. Designed to be inefficient on ASIC miners	No, with no end in sight. ASIC dominant.
Fair Launch	Yes	Yes
Private	Yes, 100% private by default. Optional transparency for those specific use cases Refer to chapter 3 for full details on privacy	No privacy on Layer 1 chain Partial privacy in upper layers
Adoption rate	<1%	1-5%
Provides freedom	Yes. Unrivalled.	I would argue largely yes.

In the next part of this chapter, we will look at the specific areas FUD (Fear, uncertainty & doubt) rather than the areas of comparison that we have looked at so far.

The following are arguments frequently voiced mainly by Bitcoin maximalists:

Unauditable supply

The accusation of an unauditable supply is probably the most common argument against Monero. In essence, they are claiming that the total circulating supply of Monero is not and cannot be known.

An argument that is factually untrue and mostly based on intellectual laziness.

I have subsequently taken the liberty (with permission) to copy and paste Seth's response to this FUD to preserve the beauty of the intended message.

Seth's response to Monero having an unauditable supply is as follows:

"Monero's supply can be easily audited by anyone running a Monero node, but this process does rely on the soundness of the "monerod" software implementation (which is the name of the software), and the validity of cryptography used in "range-proofs".

These "range-proofs" allow it to be mathematically proven that the inputs and outputs of each transaction add up to zero without revealing amounts, ensuring that the supply is sound and not inflated in any way.

Every node on the network is validating these range-proofs in each transaction every time a transaction is first seen, and validating all historical range-proofs when initially syncing.

A manual audit is possible because Coinbase transactions (the transactions that are mining rewards in each block including issuance + transaction fees) are intentionally transparent and the amounts of these outputs are not obfuscated in any way.

Monero users running a node can simply validate these totals on-demand, and all node owners are constantly verifying the amounts in transactions via range-proofs.

Unlike Bitcoin, however, Monero users cannot simply do "napkin math" and validate the supply by manually adding up UTXO amounts, as transactions are never known-spent by the network, only by the parties involved in each specific transaction.

This does force some added reliance on code/cryptography over Bitcoin, but as-of-yet I know of no one validating the Bitcoin supply this way.

It does remain a valuable advantage of a transparent cryptocurrency, though it comes at the cost of the transactional privacy of every user in the system."

Game, set, match, Seth.

It's important to note that while the supply relies on the correct implementation (code is not corrupt), so does all crypto's in one way or another for many different things.

Elliptic curve cryptography on Bitcoin as an example. You have to trust that the elliptic curve has not been compromised. Both of which are tried and trusted cryptographic methods which have been around for decades.

Monero is inflationary, meaning it isn't as good of as a store of value as Bitcoin (Soft cap supply vs hard cap supply)

Firstly, it's important to note that no money in history has ever had a hard cap supply, this within itself provides evidence that it is not strictly necessary to have a "hard cap" supply. That's point number 1.

Is a hard cap supply ideal?

Maybe... Probably but look at the real world.

A money needs to work in reality, not just in theory. The inflationary supply dynamics and design of Monero is intentional.

What is provided by the linear tail emission is a guarantee that the blockchain can be mined and transactions can be processed forever, without costing $10,000 in fees. As will likely be the cost on Bitcoin once there are no more block rewards since block rewards make up 98.5% of miner income.

Why is this important and more important that a strict hard cap supply?

The only other option to avoid $10,000 fees is scaling in layers. By scaling in layers without a base block reward you create the problem you are trying to solve, which is centralization and trust.

Scaling in layers inevitably leads to huge centralisation which is ultimately trust and mutability in a game theoretical sense given enough time to play out.

This means that only a select few have the "privilege" of being able to settle their transaction on the base chain and that means that only a select few can truly own their own money.

Given that any chain including Bitcoin won't be workable once the block reward runs out, this shows us that the only option for the new type of money being cryptocurrency is to have some sort of tail emission to economically incentivise miners to secure the chain.

Realistically too, zoom out and realise the true impact of the "inflation". The tail emission began in 2022 is 0.6 XMR per block, with a current supply of 18,400,000 coins, that means that inflation at the beginning of the tail inflation is 0.87%.

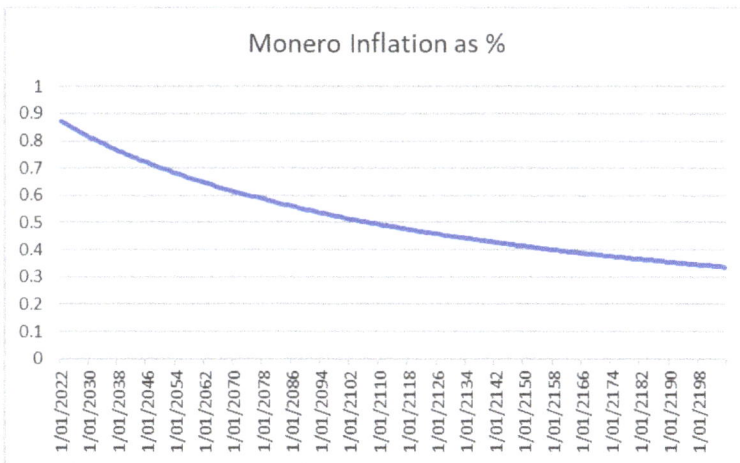

Monero Inflation as %

Because the inflation is linear and not a set certain percentage of current supply, as time goes on, the new coins produced represent a continually smaller amount of new supply vs existing supply, meaning inflation as a percentage becomes smaller and smaller over time and asymptomatically approaches 0% (it can technically never hit 0.00%).

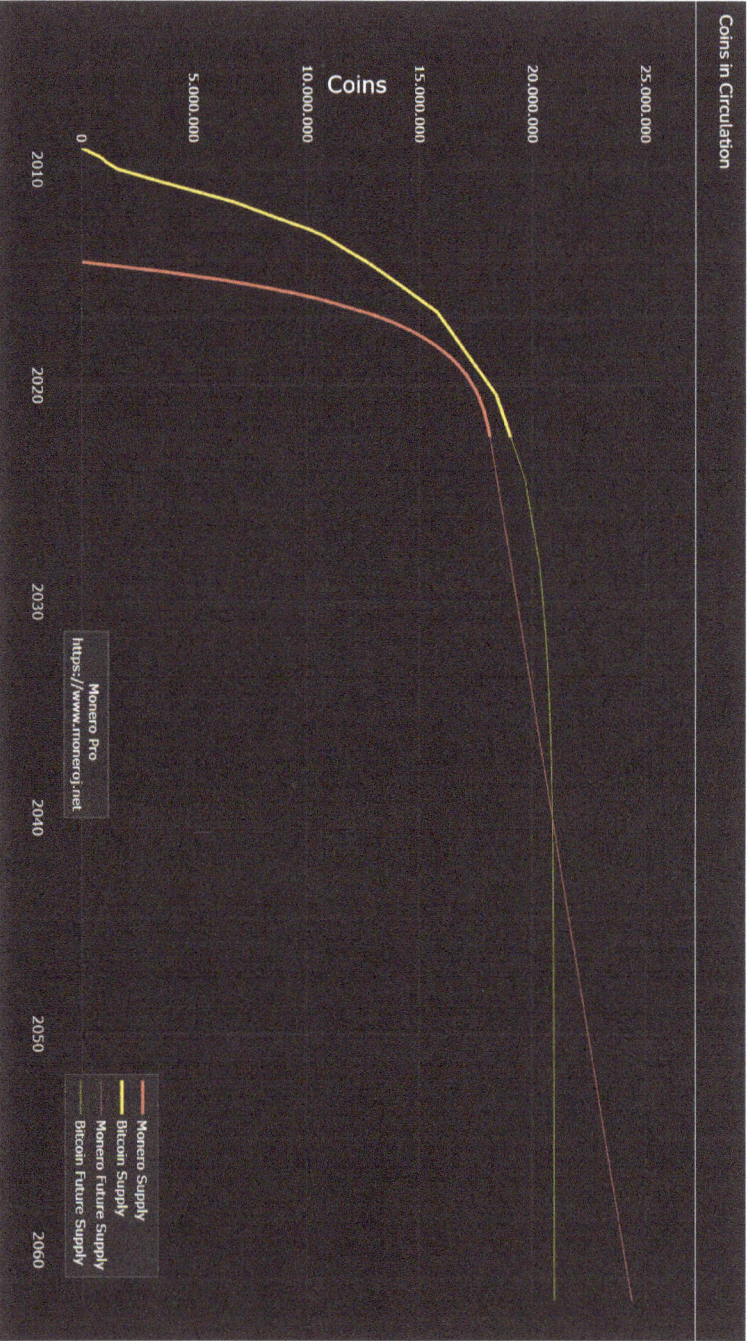

Coins in Circulation

Coins

25.000.000
20.000.000
15.000.000
10.000.000
5.000.000
0

2010   2020   2030   2040   2050   2060

Monero Pro
https://www.moneroj.net

Monero Supply
Bitcoin Supply
Monero Future Supply
Bitcoin Future Supply

This mean that the supply of Monero is technically "disinflationary" or "asymptomatically approaching 0% inflation". With enough time, inflation hits to a point of where becomes irrelevant vs current supply.

The inflation rate also lower than any money that has ever been used, including gold.

It's also important to realize that a low inflation rate of Monero is a way to replace the coins lost over time through lost wallets etc (approx. 1.5% of coins in circulation are lost every year, compared to Monero's current inflation rate of 0.87 as of writing).

It's extremely important to make it clear that the main problem with fiat currency is the arbitrary nature of the inflation/monetary policy and how the inflation is distributed per se. Not strictly that it is inflationary. As mentioned, gold & every other money ever has been Inflationary.

The problem with fiat is that the government essentially prints money and gives the money to itself for providing no value at all whilst at the cost of everyone else, whereas Monero's supply is pre-defined, verified and enforced via consensus, and entirely predictable, just like Bitcoin's.

You can know the inflation rate and total supply at any point in the future without doubts (assuming the code is correctly implemented, which we know it is at this point in time as it's based on decades old trusted cryptography used to design many other systems in systems and mathematical models in society that have been proven to work).

This tail emission enables two key features in Monero

A lower bound of network security forever (miners will always be able to rely on 0.6XMR per block, no matter the fee market)

A dynamic block size (Monero's blocks can grow/shrink to adapt to short-term increases in usage, with a penalty to mining rewards during these times).

See "Dynamic Block Sizes" for a full explanation.

The Government will ban Monero

The government will, in my opinion, almost certainly ban Monero.

With that said, when a new monetary system is created and is designed to totally reshape society. Pushback can and should be expected. It is just a sign that it is working as intended.

As a historical point, every revolution and revolutionary technology that totally disrupts the current power structure is made illegal on its road to adoption.

Considering this, if they make Monero illegal but not Bitcoin, what does this mean?

In any case, whether or not it is made illegal is mostly irrelevant. The blockchain will continue to run, the users can continue to send and receive XMR for any good or service without consequence and miners cannot be subverted or shut down as they can be on Bitcoin.

Monero is not decentralised/Hard forks from developers

Monero used to hard fork every 6 months for alleged security reasons, not anymore. Monero only forks for upgrades to the protocol.... Like Bitcoin.

In regard to the developers having influence over the forks, the thing to remember here is that people always have moved and always should move to the monetary network that provides the most value to them as a user.

No monetary system should be forced on any monetary users.

Do developers work on the protocol?

Yes, but they do in Bitcoin too.

Do they control the protocol or force upgrades/Hard forks?

Absolutely not and neither do they in Bitcoin.

Monero is totally decentralised, no single person or group of people can control it, nor can they control what version of nodes are run.

The important factor to realise is that like Bitcoin, the protocol is run and governed by the individual nodes that validate the network. Not by any individual, corporation or government. Or "federation" as a word new to Bitcoiners.

Like Bitcoin, developers in the core team do no decide what version of the protocol the validator nodes choose to run.

That is fundamentally what makes a protocol decentralised, is the ability to choose and interact with the monetary protocol that best suits your needs. Unlike fiat today. Where funnily enough, you are either not allowed in or not allowed out.

Speaking from a social influence perspective. Similarly, to Bitcoin core (the Bitcoin development team), Monero core developers probably have some influence over what version of software ends up being chosen by the validator's nodes because it's just human nature to search externally for answers and knowledge. No human can be an expert on every subject therefore we must in some sense rely on knowledge from others in every walk of life.

However, as a principle, all you can do is design a system that does not limit the freedom of the people through any centralised decision making process. That is exactly what both Bitcoin and Monero provide.

Monero has yet to have a contentious hard-fork, showing strong community support for every hard-fork so far, as the community and validator nodes have decided the hard-fork upgrades provide the most benefits for their monetary network.

People can and do run whatever nodes they want.

People can and do run nodes for the monetary network that provides he most value to them.

No liquidity/Low dollar price/Low market cap

All these arguments are different variations of the same maths.

For me, this is a sign that Monero is working. When we look at why a low price exists, we see that governments around the world have banned Monero being bought/sold on centralised exchanges in their respective countries. This by the simple maths of it severely restricts inflows of capital into the asset and especially capital from large multi-billion or trillion dollar players.

Ask the question, who are they worried about if they have banned Monero, but they haven't banned Bitcoin?

If they can catch anyone they want who transacts on the dark net in BTC and they can't catch anyone through Monero, which one works better as a freedom money? And as an extension, which one works better as an immutable money?

My second thought on this argument is that price is a distraction from the fundamental value of Monero.

Price is used as a distraction to keep the moon boys from discovering the true value of the weapon that is Monero, instead they go to other coins like Shiba, doge, NFT's or even Bitcoin.

1 XMR = 1 XMR... always, unlike Bitcoin funnily enough.

Price is nothing but a distraction from the real goal of crypto. Which is a peer to peer electronic cash system... digital cash.

Coin Joins make Bitcoin private.

Coin joins within themselves are:

1) Prohibitively expensive
   a. When talking using coin joins as a common mechanism to obscure data, they become prohibitively expensive. Here's Why:

   > 1 Transaction in
   > + 1 Transaction out
   > = 2 transactions
   > = 2 Fees ($10-$20 if you're lucky)

   b. To use coin joins as common practice would require the mixing of funds on a regular basis which could cost in the thousands of dollars per year. And that doesn't even include sending your coins to anyone else for purchases.

   c. Compare this to Monero, transactions almost always cost below 1c USD, and no mixing is required… ever…. Even if there's a fire.

2) Coinjoins do not remove data, they add it:
   a. Coin joins work by 10 people sending their coins to an address, then essentially sending those coins to new predetermined address that are not linked to known users.
   b. The theory is that by mixing the UTXO's and then sending to a new address that analytics companies and adversarial actors cannot determine the owners of the new wallets.
   c. The theory of adding data to obfuscate is not the same as removing data like is done on Monero. All it does is paint an extra target on your head since your behaviours stand out from the rest of the crown.

3) Coinjoins are easily detectable and black listable by regulators/miners.
   a. Coin joins transactions themselves are easily detectable by chain surveillance. Because the process itself is quite unique and not representative of other normal financial behaviours, it is very easy for analytics companies and adversarial actors to identify those engaging in those transactions and either:
      i. Blacklist the transaction/address'.
      ii. Go directly for the people who are engaging in such activities via KYC'd wallets etc as is done currently.

4) Coinjoins require trust in others.
   a. As an example: if because of KYC, they know who you are (otherwise you wouldn't need to mix fund) then your privacy after the mix is depending on what others do with their coins. For example, if there are 10 unknown output address (as there is 10 people in a transaction) but 1 person sends it to a KYC exchange, instead of the anonymity set being 1/10 as was the case, it now becomes 1/9 meaning that your privacy is dependent on others essentially not being stupid. Given a long enough period (the rest of ever) what are the odds that people will be will not be stupid?

Speaking of the fight back against Bitcoin, whether it be banning it, censoring transactions etc, I would predict that after CBDC's are introduced and people start shifting to CBDC's, the governments and reserve banks around the world will have to start acting.

Regulators and Chain analytics companies already often talk about the ability to identify and censor transactions. As we see on ETH, transactions can be easily censored when mining is largely centralized, like we see on both ETH and BTC today. Again, it's actually the privacy by default that Monero provides and the CPU based mining infrastructure that allows it to avoid the problems of BTC and ETH.

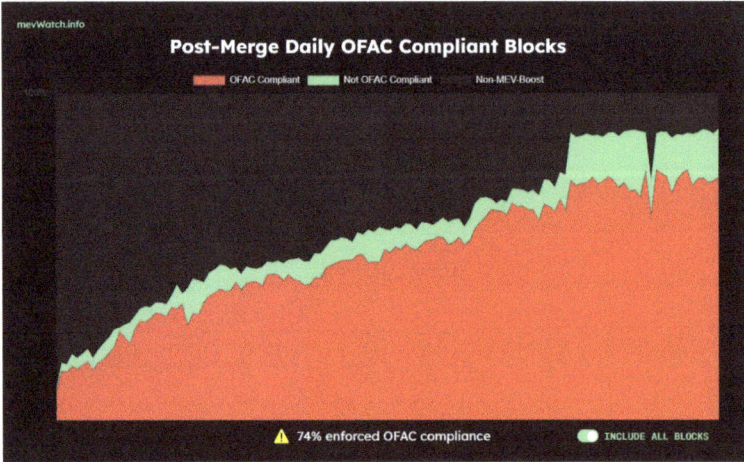

The only solution to the fungibility problems of crypto is privacy by default, as privacy is the only way to achieve true fungibility. Since the miners can't see address', the coins nor any identifying data. They can only verify the validity of transactions based on ring signatures.

To further this home, coin joins have an Anonymity set of 10, meaning there are 10 participants (including you) who all essentially pay into an address and receive random coins to another address. In Monero is the anonymity is 17, meaning that there are 17 signatures in the ring. So even if your privacy didn't rely on other people in Coinjoins, the anonymity set is still higher in Monero. Additionally, Monero, unlike Bitcoin doesn't leak any other data such as amounts etc.

There is just no possible way to justify the privacy of Bitcoin as even close to acceptable let alone safe over the long term.

Not scalable because uses more data.

To say it "can't" scale because it uses more data, shows a distinct lack of understanding of the exponential growth of technology also known as Moore's Law

The funny part of this claim is that the upgrades that Monero has adopted are specifically designed to make it the most scalable digital money long term (at least scalable whilst being genuinely decentralized).

Bitcoin was designed with 1mb as 1mb was the amount of data that 1) could handle the amount of data being sent over the network (transactions) and 2) would leave to the lowest possible hardware requirements meaning that the most amount of people could join the network... Lower barriers to entry mean more people enter.

Since Bitcoin was introduced the capability of general hardware has increased 3200%, speaking conservatively. This means that the price to enter the network has also exponentially decreased. The cost of hardware for 1mb blocks in 2009 is the same as the cost for hardware to support 32mb blocks today. Whilst technology grows exponentially, Bitcoins blockchain grows linearly, meaning that Bitcoin has failed in account for advancements in human technology and the exponential ease of people to enter networks.

An incredibly important aspect of Monero's scalability is in regard to dynamic block sizes, the block can expand and shrink where needed to fully accommodate any volume of transactions. Unlike Bitcoin where once the block is full, you have to wait till the next one which leads to a competitive price structure that has led to exorbitant transaction fees.

For full detail, see *dynamic block sizes* in chapter 6.

It's important to note that when conducting coin join transactions, the transaction size is actually larger than a Monero transaction.

In addition, when talking about scaling, anything can technically scale to any level. The main question is about decentralization in scaling. Depending on what qualitative and quantitative metrics someone puts on "decentralized" really determines whether it can "scale in a decentralized way".

Decentralization is tied to economic cost

This is mostly true; the decentralization of a network is tied to the fact of how economically difficult it is to "attack" or in other words, how economically difficult it is to make centralized.

The fact that there is more hashing power on Bitcoin is rather irrelevant when miners are highly centralized so that regulators can enforce any regulation/rules they want on them.

There is no need to attack from the outside with sustained overwhelming hash power when you can just get the miners to enforce the rules you want.

Essentially, attackers don't need hash power directly, when they can obtain it indirectly and avoid the whole "tied to economic cost" argument. We see this on Ethereum today with the OFAC compliant blocks.

Bitcoins mining process is highly centralized with ASIC farms in a small select few countries (where electricity is cheap) therefore with the threat of kicking in the doors of miners, a majority of the hash power can be "corrupted" to enforce blacklists.

On the contrary, since Monero is mined by individuals and the CPU's (computers) there are no doors to kick down besides everyone's. It would economically be impossible to enforce regulations on Monero Miners.

Bitcoin is the original, there is no need for others.

I'm going to go on the counter offensive here to reassert a fact that many Bitcoiners have overlooked or at least decided not to include in their narrative.

Bitcoiners love mentioning Satoshi when it fits their narrative i.e., that Satoshi never mentions blockchain. But they don't want to admit certain things that Satoshi said when it doesn't fit their narrative like the fact that Satoshi never called the infrastructure a time chain.

Satoshi's original ambition was "Peer to Peer Electronic cash system". This is literally the title of the Bitcoin whitepaper.

This logically indicates that the aim of Bitcoin is to be a peer to peer electronic cash system, pretty simple, right?

Cash however is fungible... Bitcoin is not.

Monero is a far superior digital cash system than Bitcoin. Cash is private and cash in fungible.

Bitcoin is not private and as we discussed earlier, Bitcoin is not fungible.

Monero is private and Monero is 100% fungible.

Making it not only a much better representation of Satoshi's original goal of creating a true digital cash. But we need to admit that there is a need for another because Bitcoin has failed to do what it says in the title on the front page.

Chapter 8

The Monero Standard

Freedom, Privacy And The Groundwork For Prosperity

I would now like to stack up the cards in an easy to understand way.

1) Fiat money is not real money.

2) The fiat monetary system benefits only those closest to the monetary spigot. In short, the elites that play with our lives and those who use the spigot to enrich themselves at our expense.

3) Fiat is a Ponzi. Fiat is mathematically going to collapse with or without reform, be that in a literal sense or at minimum, in a purchasing power sense to where fiat goes so close to 0 that it becomes worthless.

4) An alternative monetary system will be needed either by the fact that the current system does not serve the interest of the people who use it but rather by the 0.001% of people who design it or by the fact that fiat is a Ponzi that will collapse or both reasons. In any case, you will need a new system.

5) Reform cannot change the system, even if fiat wasn't a Ponzi.

6) Revolutionary cycles are all converging now to provide a platform for natural revolutionary change.

7) 50 Year Technological Revolution, 80 Year Political/societal Revolution & 250 Year empire Revolution cycles are all converging.

8) Short and long term debt cycles are converging.

9) Generational cycles are converging.

10) The global power structure has immense power to implement their outlined socialist dystopian agendas by control of Money, politics & information.

11) A future filled with technocracy and globalism will only serve to increase centralization, reduce individual liberty, serve to benefit the very few elites closest to the money spigot & reduce the prosperity of the average person.

12) Extreme efforts will be made by the current global power structure to keep their manipulated place at the top of the food chain.

13) Any effort to deplatform the global power structure by rug pulling their control over the money will be met with stiff militant resistance.

14) The solution to technocracy and globalism is the decentralisation and privatization of systems that are being used to form power structures.

15) Summed up, the 2 main problems are Fiat & Technocracy/Globalism.

16) The solution to fake fiat money is hard PoW money that has real value and cannot be manipulated.

17) The solution to technocracy/globalism are privacy tools & technologies that cannot be stopped (mathematics).

18) The method of maths that counters the current and future weapons of the global power structure should be used to achieve the best results.

19) Combining all those needs, Monero is that method. Monero is decentralized, Private PoW Money.

20) Monero provides the best basis we have ever had as a species for long lasting freedom and equality of opportunity.

The important note to take away from stacking all the cards in a simple easy to understand manner is "T.I.N.A" aka there is no alternative. If we, both personally and socially want a world where we have, at minimum have a some level of privacy in any form and ultimately freedom of choice, we need to 1) separate money from state and 2) that money needs to have all the attributes that fight against the socialist and dystopian agendas that threaten privacy and freedom.

So how do we move to a Monero standard?

As of where we are at the moment, it is a long road ahead. With it being such a long road ahead, it is a road full of opportunity there for the taking. Every challenge is an opportunity is disguise.

We cannot expect any help from the globalists, as those banning Monero from exchanges, allowing the creation of fake "paper" Monero on exchanges and doing everything they can to stop it, are the ones directly benefiting from creating a fake dollar and being able to print money (which is ultimately influence and power) out of thin air. We must make and adopt a Monero standard in society by ourselves... The ultimate peaceful revolution that provides a long lasting platform for freedom and prosperity, without firing a single shot.

The fightback against Monero is a sign that we are on the right path, if they are trying to stop Monero but allow Bitcoin and the tens of thousands of other shitcoins, what does that mean?

The answer is obvious.

A change to a Monero standard will have many steps and events on the road. Predictable results will play out in an unpredictable manner.

In fact, contrary to their best efforts, the road to a Monero standard is already unintentionally being paved, mostly by globalists and those with malicious intentions. They are creating demand for forces that go against their socialist and dystopian agenda's.

The road to a Monero standard, as with revolutionary cycles, is a process, not an event. Therefore, it is only natural that things play out over longer periods of time rather than all happening at once or having happened already.

The base technology is already here and the factors that will drive people towards it are only going to become more exacerbated and pronounced as time goes on.

There are really 1,000,000 things that need to be done:
1) Build community of users
   a. A cultural homebase (like El Salvador for BTC)
   b. More Books about Monero
   c. Academic level courses
   d. More XMR YouTube Videos
   e. Lobby politicians to make Monero friendly laws
   f. Onboard new users
   g. Host more events
   h. Run full nodes
   i. Commit hash power to the network.

2) Web apps that's use Monero
   a. Browser Wallet
   b. Easy UX Wallet
   c. Atomic swaps
   d. Defi Bridges
   e. Monero Only exchanges
   f. Big tech resistant wallets
   g. Monero First/Dominated Exchanges
   h. Integration into other web applications
   i. Subscription Payment Applications

3) Circular Economy
   a. IRL places that accept Monero
   b. Wholesalers and Manufacturers accepting XMR
   c. Wages paid in Monero
   d. Commodities priced in Monero
   e. Taxes Paid in Monero
   f. Spend Monero on:
      i. Food
      ii. Rent
      iii. Healthcare
      iv. Goods
      v. Services
      vi. Community tipping in the economy
   g. Accept Monero in your business
   h. Monero/Privacy focused VC's
   i. XMR GoFundMe Alternatives
   j. Monero Patreon Alternatives.
   k. Monero Market Places like eBay/Amazon
   l. Monero Classified Like Craigslist/Gumtree
   m. Monero payment rail and solution companies like Square
   n. Monero/privacy focused companies
   o. Partnering with human rights organisations & NGO's to highlight positive aspects of privacy

These are only a few of the things that need to be done, there are 1,000,000 ideas beyond this that will help the community and the adoption of Monero to grow. Which ultimately means freedom and prosperity growing. To pretend I have the knowledge to centrally plan everything that needs to be done is the exact naivety that Monero is fighting against.

With there being so much to be done, each and every one of you can benefit from this in so many ways by participating in one or many of the opportunities mentioned. It is an opportunity to not only set yourself up in the Monero space but to also build business that can benefit you, consumers, and society overall.

If that's not the opportunity you are after, then I'm not sure how you made it this far in the book but fair play, nevertheless.

External events that will play out to help push the probability of the everyday person needing or wanting to use Monero are, in no particular order:

1) Continued adoption on dark net and Black Markets/adoption where freedom seeking people are focused.
2) Cash to be banned.
3) CBDCs to be introduced to control what people can buy and sell based on a social/carbon credit score.

4) Digital ID's
5) Social/carbon credit systems used to limit economic and social behaviours based on scores.
6) "Cyber Pandemic"
7) KYC Internet
8) Increasing concerns about personal/business privacy
9) Commonly desired goods to be banned like meat.
10) Bitcoin and transparent protocols to be heavily regulated, tracked and manipulated.
11) More people to be discriminated against for events such as Canadian trucker protest and Dutch farmer protests
12) Adoption in small nations
13) Adoption as legal tender
14) Taxes paid in Monero
15) Extreme volatility in markets as law makers become increasingly irrational and desperate.

As I mentioned, these are just a few examples of what will likely drive the broad adoption of Monero. Each event is not strictly necessary to play out nor are they the only things that will or need to play out. But rather, they are a broader principle of what is likely to play out, being actions that facilitate the continuation of the encroachment of personal freedom, privacy and ultimately quality of life.

Each step that encroaches on one of these factors ultimately increases the likelihood that someone is going to search for alternatives and as we have discussed already, the best alternative for long lasting freedom, privacy, and prosperity is Monero.

What will certainly play out is the adoption cycle which has played out for all monies up until this date. They are:

1) Collectable – This is when a good is valued collectively by enough people, it become a collectable i.e., Fine Art

2) Store of value – When something becomes a collectable, it can the progress to become a store of value when enough people collectively value it for a long enough period of time.

The important monetary characteristics that drive its use as a store of value are limited supply and durability. Gold is an example of this.

3) Medium of exchange – Once something becomes a store of value, it can progress to becoming a medium of exchange if it once again fills the right criteria. To be a medium of exchange, the important characteristics are to be portable, divisible and fungible. Silver is a good example of this, silver was used where gold failed. Ultimately, paper notes were used where metals failed.

4) Unit of account – A unit of account implies that it is widely recognised by all and is seen as to be the most commonly held most saleable asset. Gold is an example of this and even by extension the gold florin that was used between 1252 – 1533.

Obviously, not all assets that start at the collectable stage end up moving down the chain to become a store of value etc, however every money goes through these stages on its way to becoming a widely adopted money besides fiat (which instead, is simply by decree).

Monero was a collectable for nerds in the early days.

Monero has surpassed the store of value stage as it has proven to be an immutable and uncensorable store of value for many people living under adversarial conditions around the world. Bitcoin Maxi's will argue that because it has no hard cap that it cannot be a store of value, a claim that is false. Whilst it is not adopted as a wide store of value at this stage, it has proved to have the attributes that any good store of value will need such as scarcity, known value and privacy.

Like normal technology, Monetary technology too, is emergent on the fringes and the fringes are choosing Monero.

This is the signal, not the noise.

It is my contention that we are currently at the beginning of the medium of exchange phase since Monero is used on the fringes on the DarkNet almost exclusively. Monero also has properties that make it the best digital cash we have ever seen as we discussed earlier in the book.

We must come together and unite as a community of not only "Monero bro's" but also as hard money maximalists, freedom maximalists, libertarians and just all people who place any value whatsoever of freedom of choice and prosperity, to create circular economies and do everything we can to have long lasting, freedom & prosperity enabling hard money broadly used and accepted. This is what will turn Monero into a unit of account.

Monero is our only hope.

With all this said, **what does life look like on a Monero standard?**

Philosophically, money is ultimately the purest form of expression. Through analysing financial transactions, we can ultimately analyse societies preferences for what we as humans truly value in an unhindered way.

We can analyse what as a society, we like, don't like, what we find beautiful, what human behaviours are common or probable, even other things like what people eat, what modes of transport are most advantageous, what religions you believe should be practised.

Essentially, in a free environment, money is freedom of speech. Money is freedom. Don't worry though, personal data is not possible because Monero is private. We would be able to observe this by observing society as a whole. When ideas are competing in a free market with free money, we can see what ideas are valued and ultimately, we have the power to live a life as free and prosperous as possible. Money is the ultimate vote and we use it to implement and support the world we see fit. This isn't a 1 sided thing where those with the most money get the most power but quite the opposite where you need to provide the most value to others in order to obtain money.

We see a society where relationships between parties are completely redefined to a completely consensual basis, parties will only interact when there is a mutual benefit or at minimum mutual consent. It brings freedom back to the individual and truth back to the overall market, unlike the distorted markets today, where the freshest printed dollars being funnelled into whatever industry deemed fit to fit the political or economic narrative of the day.

When we have:

1) Taken the money out of the hands of centralized authority (PoW)
2) Become resistant to dystopian agendas and attacks in a long term game theoretical sense (Privacy)

We can see a vast array of changes within society, and a change in a vast number of behaviours that will take place. Behaviours associated with true rights and true responsibilities.

Essentially, having these 2 characteristics in money puts purity and prosperity back into our society. It totally changes society as a whole. We have obviously discussed in chapter 5 many of the benefits of a PoW Money.

Monero separates money and state forever.

Now as we mentioned at the start of the book, you can see why
Monero truly sets the world free and puts humanity on a course for
long lasting freedom and prosperity for the first time in human history.

Epilogue

If you have made it this far, I want to take this opportunity to firstly thank you from the bottom of my heart for putting in the effort to read the book. Ultimately, because you have gained this information, you can now go out and weaponize it to Monero pill either some Bitcoiners, shitcoiners, no coiners and/or normies.

Believe it or not, this book took me well over 2000 Hours in reading, researching, talking and writing to make it to these final few sentences.

I would like to take this opportunity to ask for a donation if you feel I have provided value to you, to the Monero community and to the world.

83SgwgMqLw8fgpEKvH6eXt8cDYfoNGBuK2non7ZyGF3xGKrvJb19dSr5 1NwKExsLWfSShsP9DMvKf4eGrvX9TsfQGTsiCS8

Any and all amounts are appreciated much more than you know… If $1 is all you can afford, as I say, I appreciate it more than you know.

In all seriousness, I'm actually a pretty open guy. I don't have anything to hide so feel free to reach out via Twitter @TheStoicCoiner if you have any questions or need any help. My DMs are always open for Monero plebs.

I love Monero and I love freedom.

Together we can change the world and I am not just saying that…just do the maths on network effects.

But with that said, it means you need to do your part too. Look at this very individualistically… Do what you can and everything you can do… This world is in a dire situation, and we need people like you… The remnant… to fix it. Without people like you standing up and being counted, we are all screwed anyway so you may as well do it.

What you can do for the world:

1. Orange/grey pilling people you know. Even if that includes sending then a few bucks of XMR to get them set up.
2. If you own a business, accept Monero.
3. if you know someone who owns a business, get them to accept it or at least start them off by accepting it for a small amount of their products/services.
4. Make #Monero and/or #XMR big on twitter and other social platforms. Post every day with a #Monero in it. 100,000 of them per day goes pretty far pretty quickly.
5. Put those hashtags in your bio.
6. Give Monero to people as a present instead of non-productive consumable goods.
7. Lobby members of parliament/congress to legislate laws/regulations that are friendly to Monero.

God speed.

Special Mentions

As the Monero community, we need to work together.

Our counterparts in government, central banking, finance and the globalist establishments are working together on a level most people cannot comprehend.

It is only with a combined effort that we will be able to achieve our goal of providing freedom through privacy and Proof of Work (PoW) in money.

I can say that I have received a lot of help for this book from many members of the Monero community and also the broader community.

So, I would like to commend some specific members of the community for their contributions . All of whom, contributed in a way large or small. Most don't even know they contributed.

I would like to give a special mention to the following.

Uberbleu (@tony_huszar)

Bob From Monero Boating Club

Alesha Butters (@Bake_Envy_)

Vikrant Sharma (@vikrantnyc)

Nam Sardar (@Namsardar)

Luke Mikic (@LukeMikic21)

David Salazar

Sarang Noether

Seth For Privacy (@sethforprivacy)

Ricardo Spagni (@fluffypony)

Frank Cabañas aka Artic Mine

Douglas Tuman (@DouglasTuman)

Justin Ehrenhofer (@JEhrenhofer)

Mano Crypto (@mano_crypto)

Mark Moss (@1MarkMoss)

Ray Dalio (@RayDalio)

Harry Bencraft

Whitney Webb (@_whitneywebb)

Aleks Svetski (@SvetskiWrites)

Truth be told, it really was many more people than this that helped bring this book together. The entire Monero community is responsible for this. Without the community, this book would not be possible.

Keep the revolution alive fellow plebs.

Appendix

Bonds – A contract for money, generally dollars. When money is loaned to someone, a predetermined repayment is set for the Sum + interest.

Cantillon/Cantillionaire – a person that disproportionally benefits from the wealth inequalities created by central bank monetary policy.

CBDC – Central Bank Digital Currency. A digital version of fiat money that is issued by a central bank.

Centralized – Control by a single authority or managed in one place.

CPI – Consumer Price Index. A metric that governments often use as a proxy to measure inflation. CPI uses a manipulated basket of goods to measure the increase of prices. CPI is generally an inaccurate method for calculating the true extent of rising costs.

Credit – Goods or services obtained without payment with the faith of future payment. The same concept as a bond.

Decentralized – Controlled by several distributed authorities. No one authority has power.

DEI – Diversity, equity, and inclusion refers to organizational frameworks which seek to promote "the fair treatment and full participation of all people", particularly groups "who have historically been underrepresented or subject to discrimination" on the basis of identity or disability.

Dystopia – an state or society in which there is great suffering or injustice, typically one that is totalitarian. Typically, one thinks they are moving towards a utopian society however they realise it's the opposite when it is too late.

ESG – Environmental, Social and Governance scores are used to screen investments based on corporate policies and to encourage companies to "act responsibly".

Fiat – Literally means "by decree". It refers to money which has value simply because the government has decreed that it has value. In other words, the paper money we use today.

Fiduciary Responsibility – A fiduciary is a person who holds a legal or ethical relationship of trust with one or more other parties (person or group of persons). Typically, a fiduciary prudently takes care of money or other assets for another person. A fiduciary responsibility is a legal responsibility to in essence look out for the best interests of the person/people whose money/assets they're managing/directing.

Inflation – Increase of the Monetary supply. Prices rise due to inflation.

Keynesian – A school of economic theory devised by John Maynard Keynes. A Theory that advocates for central planning of markets and government intervention in markets.

KYC – Know Your Customer. A regulatory framework in which consumers/investors are required to submit identity documents to confirm who they are. Generally justified with the narrative of "anti-money laundering" & "Counter Terrorism".

Legislation – An act of parliament/congress to implement a law.

Malthusian - Malthusianism represents a form of economic pessimism that challenges utopian notions of the perfectibility of human societies.

Mining - Mining refers to the process where a computer runs the code to ensure that transactions are cryptographically legitimate. Mining is also how new coins are entered into circulation.

Monetary Spigot – A spigot is a device to turn on or off water. A monetary spigot euphemism for an entity/object that controls the supply of money.

Monetary Supply – The money supply is the sum total of all of the currency and other liquid assets in a country's economy on the date measured.

Normie – A normal person. Specifically, A person not interested in "crypto".

Orwellian – reference to George Orwell's dystopian account of a future totalitarian state in "Nineteen Eighty-Four".

Panopticon – The panopticon is a design of institutional buildings. The concept is to allow all prisoners of an institution to be observed by a single security guard, without the inmates knowing whether they are being watched.

Although it is physically impossible for the single guard to observe all the inmates' cells at once, the fact that the inmates cannot know when they are being watched motivates them to act as though they are all being watched at all times. They are effectively compelled to self-regulation.

Pre-mine – A design which is used to obtain a % of the supply without having to use the methods in which others have to use such as mining. A/the developer/s will often premine some of the supply to themselves when designing a cryptocurrency protocol, this is often so they can sell their coins later for financial gain. A pre-mine is often considered "scammy".

Ponzi – A Ponzi scheme is a form of fraud that lures investors and pays profits to earlier investors with funds from more recent investors.

Proof of Stake (PoS) – A mechanism for selecting who process' transactions and blocks in a cryptocurrency network. Participants are generally selected proportionately based on how many coins they have "staked" i.e., locked up in a node.

Proof of stake is also a governance mechanism for a crypto protocol where participants have influence based on how many coins they have. A replication of the current political system.

Proof of Work (PoW) – Proof of work is a cryptographic method of verifying transactions and blocks where you are required to provide real world resources that are limited in their creation, such as hashing power.

Reserve Currency – A currency that is held by most if not all nations and is used to facilitate global trade and credit due to the confidence that everyone universally values it more than any other currency.

Shitcoiner – Typically someone who advocates for cryptocurrencies other than Bitcoin. In the book, we use it to refer to people who advocate for pre-mined and/or Proof of stake coins.

The Great Reset –An "economic recovery plan" devised by the World Economic Forum (WEF) in response to the COVID-19 pandemic. The plan involves implementing "stakeholder capitalism".

Unfunded Liabilities – A debt for which there is no current or projected assets to pay for it.

Utopia - an imagined place or state of things in which everything is perfect. The opposite of dystopia.

www.ingramcontent.com/pod-product-compliance
Lightning Source LLC
Chambersburg PA
CBHW040848210326
41597CB00029B/4776